NATIONAL SOCIALISM:
Vanguard of the Future

Selected Writings of Colin Jordan

NATIONAL SOCIALISM:
Vanguard of the Future

Selected Writings Of Colin Jordan

© N.S. Press (U.K)

NATIONAL SOCIALISM:
Vanguard of the Future
Selected Writings of Colin Jordan

First published by
NORDLAND FORLAG
AALBORG 1993

This Third edition 2021

ISBN 978-1-899765-23-2   Hardback
ISBN 978-1-899765-24-9   Paperback

INTRODUCTION	**5**
I. The Past: Adolf Hitler and National Socialist Germany	**9**
1. Hitler Was Right!	10
2. Adolf Hitler: The Man against Time	18
3. Adolf Hitler: Man of the Century	22
4. The Enemy Within	25
5. Book Review: *Blood and Soil by Anna Bramwell*	33
6. Murder at Spandau	38
II: THE PRESENT: NATIONAL SOCIALISM TODAY	**50**
1. National Socialism: A Philosophical Appraisal	51
2. National Socialism: World Creed for the Future	56
III. INTO THE FUTURE: THE NATIONAL SOCIALIST VANGUARD	**77**
1. Building the Vanguard	78
2. Party Time Has Ended: The Case for Politics Beyond the Party	81
3. A Train of Thought	89
APPENDIX: Letter to Gerald Kaufman, M.P	**98**
Biographical Note	**101**

Companion Volume to this book:

The National Vanguard: The Way Forward
By Colin Jordan

INTRODUCTION

Make no mistake about it: this is a dangerous book. The ideas contained in this slim volume are explosive enough to blow the whole power structure of the Western world to smithereens. The author is a bold and eloquent exponent of the most hated, the most feared, and the most reviled creed of modern times: Adolf Hitler's National Socialism.

Contained herein in concentrated form are the most-forbidden thoughts of the post- 1945 era: praise of Adolf Hitler and the defence of his policies; the open advocacy of National Socialism for the entire White race; and a course of action whereby this goal can be attained, even against the most brutal and determined opposition.

The masters of the media are fond of portraying real-life contemporary National Socialists as though they are stock comedy villains who have escaped from some Hollywood movie. Colin Jordan puts the lie to the depiction of the National Socialist as a megalomaniacal madman, spewing mindless hate and frothing at the mouth. He is what may be described, quite precisely, as "the thinking man's National Socialist." His thoughts are logical and ordered; he has a sweeping grasp of the past, a lucid appreciation of the present, and penetrating insights into the future. At the same time, he writes with a passionate intensity that comes only to those who have absolute conviction in their beliefs. He is coolly analytical or blisteringly critical, depending on the requirements of the topic under discussion. Further, Jordan is no armchair intellectual, and when he writes of building elite National Socialist task forces to implement the "tactics of Otto Skorzeny" in the political sphere, he carries the authority of someone who speaks from first-hand experience.

Colin Jordan was born in 1923 and graduated from Cambridge University with a Honours degree in history in 1949. He began his political career in the 1940s as a protege of Arnold Leese, one of the few pre-war British National Socialists who had the courage and the stamina to continue the struggle after the defeat of 1945. Upon Leese's death, Jordan inherited his house on Princedale Road in London, which quickly became the headquarters of the White Defence League. This was the first organisation which Jordan formed, and in 1960 he merged it with other British racialist groups into the British National Party. Subsequently there was a falling out in the BNP (which is no relation to the current party of the same name) between those who favoured a hard-core advocacy of National Socialism and those who desired to take a more moderate, softer approach. Jordan, of course, led the hard-core group, and from this split came the National Socialist Movement.

As is only fitting for a National Socialist organisation, the NSM was born in struggle. It was founded on April 20, 1962, and on July 2nd of that year it held its first mass meeting in London's Trafalgar Square, underneath a forty-foot banner reading "Free Britain from Jewish Control!" Some 5,000 people attended this open-air gathering, including a mob of Jews who quickly became hysterical at the contents of Jordan's speech. The ensuing riot ended in Jordan's arrest—and not, significantly, in the arrest of his attackers. More important than his one month's jail time was the result that the NSM was henceforth not allowed to hold such public meetings. Another consequence of the battle was the decision to form a self-defence arm of the NSM—which resulted in Jordan's second imprisonment of the year. He got the message: all pretence of democracy and free speech aside, the powers-that-be in Britain were absolutely not going to allow National Socialists the same rights to organise as other political parties.

A lesser man would have been discouraged and given up the fight after such a disheartening initial nine months. Instead, Jordan adjusted his strategy and began a 12-year campaign of political guerrilla warfare by way of propaganda against the British establishment. Perhaps the most striking example of these NSM activities was those which contributed to the defeat of Labour candidate Gordon Walker in 1965. Walker was an outspoken advocate of non-White immigration into Britain. Through countless publicity stunts, through demonstrations, and through disrupting his meetings, Jordan kept the race-threatening nature of Walker's candidacy in the public eye. So effective were these efforts that a squad of thugs from the Jewish "62 Group" was brought in to silence Jordan. At Walker's final election meeting in Leyton Baths on January 20, 1965, they attacked Jordan, with shouts of "Kill him! Kill him! " Jordan was brutally beaten and required hospitalization. but Walker lost the election.

In 1967 Jordan was again jailed, this time for distributing two pamphlets. One of these criticized Jewish domination of British society, and the other, The Coloured Invasion, warned Britons of the perils of the flood of non-White immigration which was sweeping across their shores. Sadly, the age-old rights of native Britons had so deteriorated by this time that even the written criticism of the baleful effects of non-Britons was deemed illegal. Following his release from jail, Jordan reorganised the NSM as the "British Movement," and it continued as such until his retirement from politics in 1975.

It would take a separate volume to chronicle a complete history of British National Socialism, but there are other achievements of Jordan and the NSM that must be mentioned. During August of the eventful year 1962, Jordan hosted an international meeting of National Socialist leaders in the Cotswold, England. Among those in attendance were Lincoln Rockwell, Bruno Luedtke, and Savitri Devi. Out of this gathering the World Union of National Socialists was born, the first attempt to give international structure to the post-war movement. It should also be noted that the NSM published an occasional newspaper, *The National Socialist*, throughout its history, as well as a manifesto calling for a National Socialist state, *Britain Reborn*.

Today Colin Jordan is a youthful 68, and is a member of no organisation. His current activities consist of writing, book-selling, and publishing a newsletter, *Gothic Ripples*.

Even his enemies accord him a grudging recognition of his stature and abilities. Recently the Crown Prosecution Service described him as "the grandfather of British National Socialism." A spokesman for the Jewish Board of Deputies called Jordan "the guru of British Nazism," and the venomous "anti-Fascist" rag Searchlight denounced him as 'a real Jew-baiter,' which simply means that they find him an effective opponent of Jewish hegemony over Britain. (All quotes taken from the article "Police raid the home of leading neo-Nazi veteran," *Jewish Chronicle*, pl, June 28, 1991.)

Such are Colin Jordan's impressive political credentials. The reader must judge the impressiveness of Jordan's ideas for himself.

A word must be said about Colin Jordan's writing style, which some readers may occasionally find difficult, especially in parts two and three of this collection. These essays—especially those dealing with a course of action for the Movement—were not written for the casual amusement of armchair racialists or for those "National Socialists" who treat the battle for Aryan survival as a hobby, which they pursue at their leisure, if and when the mood strikes them. Nor are they written for those whose intellectual level can be plotted on the lower half of the IQ bell curve. No, these words were written for the elite of our race: for those who have the strength of intellect to understand the full depth of the National Socialist creed, and who at the same time have the strength of character to actively participate in the National Socialist struggle. Those few Aryans who fall into this category are the readers to whom Jordan is writing.

Nor does he desire that his words be taken lightly. These writings are not intended to be grasped in their entirety upon a single cursory perusal. Rather, the author wants his ideas studied carefully and thoroughly, in both depth and detail. Jordan desires that his target audience read these thoughts not just once or twice but again and yet again. He wants the reader to ponder over them, and to determine by himself their full ramifications. Most importantly, after the reader has fully absorbed these words and has considered their full implications, he wants these essays to serve as a basis for action.

All this is not to say that the author is incapable to expressing himself in a concise and direct manner. Quite the contrary! These essays are packed with eloquent and memorable phrases: "thinking with the blood;" "fragments of the future," "a revolution in thought;" and "applying the principles of Otto Skorzeny to political warfare" are just a few examples of Jordan's facility with striking and evocative language. When he feels the need, he can express himself in a crisp and authoritative manner that slams home key ideas in no uncertain terms: "What fulfils Nature; what benefits the race as a servant of Nature; what benefits National Socialism as a servant of the race; is good: what does not is bad. That which truly seeks and secures this good is right. That which does not is wrong. No other command to the contrary can be accepted by National Socialists."

Whatever difficulties a reader might have with the author's style is more than amply compensated for by the richness and brilliance of his ideas. These essays require time and effort and thought, but they repay the energy expended many times over. The thoughts expressed here are not going to please everyone. They are not intended to. The ruling powers in Britain will not be happy to see a collection of the writings of this most persistent and troublesome enemy of theirs. Perhaps they will ban the distribution of this book within the United Kingdom. Likewise, there are those within the racialist movement—and maybe even some who consider themselves as National Socialists—who will disagree with part of what Jordan has to say. So be it. In *Schopenhauer as Educator*, Friedrich Nietzsche explains, "I consider every word as useless behind which does not stand a call to action." Such is the attitude of Colin Jordan. If enough of the right people read this book and determine to put the ideas it contains into effect, the entire structure of the Old Order will come crashing down—and a New World for Aryan humanity will be built amid its ruins. *Editor*

I. THE PAST: ADOLF HITLER AND NATIONAL SOCIALIST GERMANY

The following six articles show the perfect blending of Colin Jordan's deep insight into National Socialism, his interest in history, and his determination to discover and proclaim the truth.

"Hitler Was Right! " are the first of three essays which appear here written to commemorate the 100th anniversary of the birth of Adolf Hitler in 1989. It is an eloquent, persuasive, and defiant defence of Hitler and his policies. It first appeared in issue 20/21 of Colin Jordan's newsletter, *Gothic Ripples*.

"*Adolf Hitler: Man, Against Time*" is the second of the commemorative pieces. It originally appeared in the NS *Bulletin*, publication of the New Order. Here Jordan follows the exposition of Savitri Devi in describing Hitler as a superhuman personality who through the force of his own will and genius sought to reverse the decay of Aryan humanity.

"*Adolf Hitler: Man, of the Century*" is the third of the centenary essays. This is a more personal appraisal of the founder of National Socialism, in which the author discusses the meaning of Hitler and the effect, he had on his own life. It is reprinted from the *League Sentinel.*

"*The Enemy Within*" answers various charges laid against Hitler and National Socialist Germany by some of those today who profess sympathy to National Socialism, but whose real sympathy only extends to Hitler's rivals, and not to the Author of the National Socialist Idea and Founder of the Movement himself. Another *Gothic Ripples reprint.*

"*Book Review: Blood and Soil*," reprinted from the National Review, reviews Anna Bramwell's biography of Walther Darre. Jordan uses the occasion to comment on National Socialist agricultural policy and to further answer criticisms of Hitler by present-day National Bolsheviks.

"Murder at Spandau," also from Gothic Ripples, discusses the background of the historic flight of Rudolf Hess, his post-war imprisonment, and his eventual murder by the British in 1987. *Editor*

National Socialism: Vanguard of the Future

HITLER WAS RIGHT!

Never in all history has a man been so vilified as he whose centenary of birth occurred on the 20th of April 1989. According to the mass media of today's democracy, he was an absolute monster, an insane incarnation of evil. However, the very fact that he is presented as so totally black, with nothing at all to his credit, should excite suspicion in anyone other than an utter idiot or some partisan blinded by prejudice.

The vilification was not always total as now. Lloyd George, British premier during World War I, after a visit to Germany in 1936, was quoted in the Daily Telegraph of 22nd September of that year as stating: "*I have never seen a happier people than the Germans. Hitler is one of the greatest men I have ever met.*" In a letter to a friend in December of that year he said: "*I only wish we had a man of his supreme quality at the head of affairs in our country today.*"

Viscount Rothermere, in his pre-war book, "Warnings and Predictions", said of Hitler: "*He has a supreme intellect... He has thoroughly cleansed the moral, ethical life of Germany. No words can describe his politeness ... He is a man of rare culture. His knowledge of music, the arts and architecture is profound.*"

The iron curtain of lies completely descended when the elements intent on destroying Hitler became virtually omnipotent, knowing that they had to do this or they would be shown to be wrong and Hitler to be right: for he stood for Aryan renaissance, and they for an old order spelling decline and death.

The real Hitler, contrary to the mad monster of the media, was a most talented and very widely read man with a phenomenal memory, an exceedingly quick grasp of essentials, a colossal will-power, along with, of course, being the most effective orator, the world has ever known: all this in the service of a cause to which he gave himself completely. He was also a charming host, a considerate and loyal friend and colleague, kind to animals, highly appreciative of the beauties of Nature, simple in his style of personal life.

Becoming imbued in his teens with a consuming sense of mission as the liberating leader of his people in the future, he knew poverty as a young man amid the unemployed of Vienna, and danger and hardship in the frontline trenches as a soldier before joining the tiny political body which under his direction was to become the power-winning NSDAP. Night after night his captivating words brought applauding audiences from a defeated and demoralised nation to their feet in new-born hope and determination. His vocal and visual inspiration, plus the plentiful perspiration of his ardent and industrious followers, constituted the means of National Socialist success, not the mythical money-bags of big business as opponents try to make out to explain away their own inferiority in charisma, ardour and effort. As the saying had it in those days, respecting the last of these three factors, the lights always burned later in the night in the offices of Hitler's party than in those of any other.

Exhibiting the burning enthusiasm and sheer hard work: "*During one month prior to national elections in 1930, for example, the Nazi Party sponsored 34,000 meetings in Germany which averaged out to be three meetings in every village town and urban neighbourhood.*" (Mothers in the Fatherland, Claudia Koonz p 69) Typical of the receptive spirit of the people during the 1932 elections NSDAP Press Chief Otto Dietrich described a meeting at Stralsund, scheduled for 8 p.m. but for which Hitler was long delayed, finally reaching the place at 2:30 a.m.: "*In the open air, and in the pouring rain, we met the crowd drenched to the skin, weary and hungry, just as they had gathered over the night and patiently waited . . . Hitler spoke to the audience as day slowly dawned...*"

There they were, 40,000 people eagerly listening at 4 o'clock in the morning after all that time and all that discomfort to the man they rightly regarded as their political saviour! Can you imagine such a turnout for such a trumpery figure of the twilight as our present premier, Margaret Thatcher?

Just try to picture the tremendous scene of rejoicing when the long hard years of struggle were rewarded, and at the end of January 1933 Hitler became Chancellor! For hours that night a river of fire flowed past his window as thousands upon thousands of his torch-bearing party comrades paraded through the streets of a reborn Berlin. The above-mentioned Claudia Koonz quotes a longstanding NSDAP member regarding that occasion: "*We wept with happiness and joy and could scarcely believe that our beloved Führer stood at the helm of the Reich ... A magnetic power radiated everywhere and eliminated the last traces of internal resistance ... We were gripped by an inexpressible joy when we saw our banners, once scorned and belittled, flying high on all public buildings.*" (p.132)

Our thesis is not and does not have to be that Adolf Hitler was absolutely perfect and never made a single mistake, for perfection, absolute perfection, is an irrelevant abstraction which belongs not to this world, and accordingly never has and never will be seen here. What precisely we do say here is that, taking everything into account, the man and his movement in championship of our race, was the closest to perfection that this world has ever seen so far, and that is enough for us. We proclaim him right because where he is said to have gone wrong is, in our estimation, so massively dwarfed by where the opposite is true. Given but six short years of peace, he, his party and his people in unison wrought a virtual miracle in that brief span. Never elsewhere in history has so much been done for Aryan survival and revival so quickly!

Hitler was right in the supreme importance he attached to the factor of race, and, consequently, his basic conception of the nation as a racial community to be protected in its ownership of its homeland, and from interbreeding with alien stock; and, furthermore, to be improved by eugenical measures. Beyond any other statesmen in any land at any time, he gave practical recognition to the superior qualities of the Aryan peoples and the need to maximise the higher holders of those superior qualities as the golden means for human upliftment. In this unique dedication, and, consequently in the bitter opposition of all those with a vested interest against the elevation of the Aryans lies the greatest single explanation of the drive to destroy and defame him.

Hitler was right in his opposition to the disruptive party game of democracy which exists to delude and to exploit the people it pretends to represent, and in his belief instead in personality and leadership and unity. In such a fusion of the folk as he achieved, where stood the need for parties other than his? Only a minute minority remained against him after 1933, although the hostile foreign media concentrated on this fragment of discontent, and not on the almost total support he received.

Hitler was right in holding and ensuring that every man in the folk community should have productive employment for the benefit both of himself and that community. When he came to power, no less than 6,014,000 were unemployed, yet by 1938 only 338,000 remained out of. work; the vast bulk of this reduction being achieved before any significant rearmament, contrary to hostile propaganda.

Hitler was right in believing in extensive social welfare for all members of the folk community. The NSDAP's "Strength through Joy" organization had by 1938 enabled over 22 million to visit theatres, over 1 8 million to attend film performances, over 5 million to attend concerts, over 3 million to attend factory exhibitions, and no less than 50 million to take part in cultural events. The organisation had 230 establishments for popular education, and through it 62,000 educational events were arranged, being attended by 10 million people.

By 1938 490,000 had been given sea cruises, and 19 million had been given land excursions, 2 1 million had taken part in sporting events. All this at a time when the democracies left millions of unemployed to rot, and those who were employed received nothing remotely comparable to such welfare.

The best-selling car in history—more than 15 million of the Volkswagen "Beetles" in over 30 countries—resulted from Hitler's project of a people's car, a small inexpensive car for the ordinary man. Connected with this, his Autobahn construction-program preceded Britain's by decades. (This and other detailed information on the stupendous achievements of Hitler's Germany is contained in the book "Hitler's Germany" by Cesare Santoro, Berlin, 1938).

National Socialism: Vanguard of the Future

Hitler was right in the importance he attached to the protection of the peasantry as vital to a thriving folk community, his measures to this end including the legislation for hereditary holdings.

Indeed, Hitler was right in so many major ways we would need far more than the whole of this Hitler centenary double issue of Gothic Ripples to catalogue them.

Hitler's revolution accomplishing all this radical reform was a bloodless one compared with either the French Revolution (whose 200th anniversary occurs this year) or the Russian Revolution of 1917. Camps for the concentration of detainees including women and children were introduced by the British during the Boer War, and conditions in them were so bad that a great number died.

Britain's wartime ally, Russia, still has concentration camps galore in which, according to even Soviet statistics, a million people are currently held. Yet it is only the German ones we endlessly hear about with every conceivable invention and exaggeration. Colin Cross in "Adolf Hitler" (Hodder & Stoughton, London, 1973) puts the peacetime peak at 26,789 in July 1933, many being held for only a matter of weeks, and most being subsequently released, and says: "Conditions in the camps were spartan but, by prison standards, there was an adequate diet and reasonable accommodation in dormitories."

Inmates were not, as so often insinuated, all poor persecuted Jews or other heroes of democracy, but included the very dregs of society: habitual criminals, pimps, perverts, despicable drunkards, perpetual beggars and work-shy parasites.

Jewish leaders in the outside world proclaimed economic and political warfare against Hitler as soon as he came to power, and set themselves to bring about a war to destroy him. Not unnaturally, therefore, when that war came about, Hitler considered Jews in general in his territories to be enemies and a threat to security,
and so he had them rounded up and placed in ghettos or camps. During the final stages of the war when Germans were enduring the most terrible conditions themselves, including hundreds of thousands of civilian men, women and children slaughtered in air raids such as that on defenceless Dresden adequate supplies were either unavailable or failed to get through to camps overcrowded by evacuation from the east, and typhus raged, this accounting for the undeniably terrible conditions found in some of them at the end of hostilities, which were, however, certainly not the result of any deliberate policy of extermination, which allegation is an atrocity of falsehood.

After the war the campaign to denigrate Hitler focused on the allegation that 6 million Jews were deliberately exterminated at some of the camps during the war, mostly by gassing with the standard delousing fumigator, Zyklon B, which was certainly

13

in general use in the camps and other places as well for its proper purpose off preventing death (by disease), not causing it.

The super-sob-story of mass extermination of Jews in gas chambers have been decisively shown to be a colossal lie by the Leuchter Report, a report by America's leading consultant on the gas chambers in American prisons who, at the arrangement of Ernst Zundel, for the purpose of his recent retrial in Canada, visited Auschwitz and took samples from the structure of the buildings alleged to have been gas chambers which, after submission to independent analysis in the U.S.A., showed conclusively that they were not so used.

Incidentally, the recent admission by the Russians themselves that over 30 million were exterminated by Stalin, Britain's and Jewry's ally against Hitler, makes the Jewish allegation against Hitler small in comparison to this very real Red holocaust.

Returning to the Germany of the 1930s, we can estimate Hitler's greatest conquest as that of the hearts of his people, for his was the most popular regime the world has ever known. His Germany was a land electrified and transmuted. Never, anywhere at any time has a whole nation been so radiant, so disposed to service as was his under his leadership. In their millions, the German people daily acclaimed Hitler as right.

Hitler was right in seeking to rectify the iniquities of the treaty of Versailles, and to unite German territories. His actions received the overwhelming support of the populations concerned. When he entered Vienna 200,000 Viennese packed the city's Heroes' Square in an ecstasy of rejoicing at what the anti-Hitler propaganda machine in Britain called an "aggression." He was similarly welcomed in the stolen territory of the Sudetenland in the synthetic state of Czechoslovakia.

Hitler tried hard and long right up to and including the very last days of peace to reach a thoroughly fair settlement with Poland regarding the latter 's German areas and inhabitants, the port of Danzig (90% German), and the detached territory of East Prussia; but this has been deliberately obscured by the deceitful Western warmongers, Britain giving a thoroughly reprehensible general guarantee to the backward state of Poland to make its reactionary regime unreasonable and bellicose, and so to bring about the desired war.

Hitler was right in the importance he set on an Anglo- German alliance which he long strove for. With it, the combination of the British Navy and the German Army could have kept the peace of the world, preserved the British Empire which Hitler greatly valued, and served as the core for a world order of the White man safeguarding civilization through world supremacy.

National Socialism: Vanguard of the Future

The British ambassador in Berlin recorded on the 26th July 1939: *"From the very beginning Hitler has always sought above all an understanding with Britain."* (*Vansittart in Office*, I. Colvin, p. 346). Indeed, a point where Hitler went wrong was when, in persistent pursuit of an Anglo-German agreement even then, he waited after the defeat of France and the debacle of Dunkirk for Britain to come to her senses, whereas, if he had invaded in July, 1940, he would almost certainly have succeeded.

Hitler was right in his conception of a New Order for Europe, conforming to ethnic realities in preference to geographical and other demarcations conflicting with those realities, and his encouragement of co-operation to common benefit, and of unity corresponding to common aims.

Hitler was right in forestalling the intended Russian attack, planned to take advantage of the European war, by launching his own attack first in June, 1941, accompanied by the European crusade against communism which he sponsored; and, had it not been for the immense material aid given to Stalin by Britain and the U.S.A., he would have undoubtedly crushed Stalin and eliminated the Soviet menace which today is only masked by the sly tactics of Gorbachev, designed to soften up the West.

As it was, we today owe it to the gigantic effort made by Germany and her allies (including all the foreign volunteers of the wonderful Waffen-SS), and encompassing the desperate defensive fighting right up to May, 1945, that the Red Army did not break through to Calais, and that the KGB is today not stationed at Dover, Durham and Dundee.

Let it be remembered with high pride that never has a cause been fought more valiantly to the utmost than the National Socialist cause of Adolf Hitler. In the battle for Nuremberg, scene of the greatest rallies the world has ever seen: *"German civilians, men, women and youths, armed themselves to stand alongside the SS in bitter street fighting in which the veteran American 45th 'Thunderbird' Division suffered heavy casualties. The fanatical SS detachments defending the infamous Nazi Congress Hall, which Adolf Hitler called the heart of Nazism, flung back nine bloody US assaults before dying to a man."* ("The Spear of Destiny", Trevor Ravenscroft, p. 335; Neville Spearman, 1971) These were our people! "In Destination Berchtesgaden" (Ian Allan Ltd, London, 1975), J.F. Turner & R. Jackson describe the rigors of the advance thus: *Aschaffenburg: German reinforcements arrived, "many of them fanatical youths of 16 and 17 who refused to surrender and had to be annihilated.' Schweinfurt: "Every small town and village on the road to Schweinfurt was fortified, every hill and wood occupied by the enemy for as long as possible, often by fanatical Nazi youths."*

Wurzburg: *"Once again, civilians joined German troops in defending their home town, retreating into the sewers and often appearing in the Americans' rear."*

In flaming Berlin heroic remnants of the foreign volunteers of the Waffen-⚡⚡, Europe's elite, fought to the last and died defending the neighbourhood of the Reich Chancellery and the Bunker where Adolf Hitler gave up his life; and while other heroes of the Hitler Youth, some only 14, succeeded in holding the bridges over the River Spree till the very last. With blood sacrifices like this as the nutrient, National Socialism's potency to survive and revive was assured.

If there is any certainty at all in this world, it is that, if ever a real champion of our folk emerges, he will be denigrated to the utmost by the forces of ruin. So, it is that it is precisely those in Britain today who are most responsible for her present ghastly condition who are most responsible for the denigration of Hitler. Those who are damaging us the most are precisely those who denigrate him the most: that is the great equation.

Hitler was right in his denunciation of democracy; this we indeed, ought to know now by our own experience in Britain today. Bruce Anderson in the *Sunday Telegraph* (29th March 1987) said Of Britain's Afro-Asian invasion: "*The voters were never consulted: if they had been we would have had no large-scale coloured immigration.*" So, whereas Hitler's dictatorship gave the people what they wanted, and preserved Germany for the German people, Britain's democracy gives the British people what they do not want and calls it "freedom".

Hitler was right in his prophecy of the darkness which would follow his defeat. As we take stock of the whole range of evils from which we currently suffer, from recurrent strikes to the mugging of elderly ladies, from drug peddling to the promotion of perversion, from subsidies to the coloured world to the degeneracy known as "rock", we take note of the fact that Hitler would not have allowed us these blessed refinements of democracy. We also take note of the fact that projections of the present coloured birth-rate in Britain show that within a hundred years we will be a minority in our own country.

Not even the most maniacal opponent of Hitler has ever accused him of wanting to make Britain black. It has been left to those opponents to bring about just that.

National Socialist resistance did not cease in 1945. One epic figure from the war who refused to renounce his belief in National Socialism, and maintained close contact with National Socialists worldwide until his death in 1982, was Hans-Ulrich Rudel. This German flying ace held a world record for 2,530 combat flights, and another for 519 enemy tanks destroyed. Single-handedly he sank the Soviet battleship Marat and two cruisers, as well as 70 supply boats. His motto was "*Verloren ist nur wer sich selbst aufgibt*" (Only he who gives up loses").

Another stalwart from the old days was Winifred Wagner, English-born daughter-in-law of the great composer, Richard Wagner. After the war a de-Nazification court convicted her of the crime of actively supporting Hitler's regime by having been his personal friend.

For this terrible offence she was sentenced to 450 days special labour service, her personal wealth was confiscated, she was forbidden to hold any public office or become a member of any political party for five years, and she was even banned from owning a motor car.

Nevertheless, when interviewed in a film in 1975 by those who tried in vain to get her to express some rejection of Hitler, this magnificent lady rounded on them with the consummate remark: "*If Hitler walked through the door today, I would be just as glad and happy to see him and have him here as ever.*"

And so, the fight has gone on, as exhibited in such recent news items regarding Germany as the jailing of Peter Naumann for 4 1/2 years for master-minding the bombing in 1979 of a television masts near Koblenz which interrupted the transmission of the program "Holocaust", and for plotting to storm Spandau Prison when Hess was still alive and imprisoned there. Likewise, the banning of the organisation Nationale Sammlung to prevent it taking part in local elections: thus, demonstrating the utter falsity of democracy in that country, where National Socialism, the wish of a German majority, has been banned since 1945. Likewise, the headline in the *Daily Telegraph* recently "Neo-Nazism 'on the rise' in West Germany."

As long as man survives on this planet, the name Adolf Hitter will be remembered with truth or with lies. It is for us in present dismal days to derive the satisfaction of bearing witness to the truth concerning him in the face of the torrent of lies. Make it your obligation to observe and mark the 101st anniversary of his birth on April 20th, 1990!

Whatever else you do on and around that date to honour his name, make sure that at 6:18 in the evening, the time of his birth, you stop in silent meditation, lighting a candle in your heart in memory of the greatest champion of the Aryan peoples — your peoples —this world has ever seen!

"What though the field be lost?
All is not lost —the unconquerable will,
And study of revenge, immortal hate,
And courage never to submit or yield:
And what is else not to be overcome?"
(from Paradise Lost by John Milton, 1608—1674)

ADOLF HITLER: THE MAN AGAINST TIME

One hundred years ago—on the 20th day of the fourth month of 1889, shortly after six in the evening—a most momentous event occurred in a small, hitherto insignificant border town in Austria. In Brannau was born that day to parents likewise insignificant a baby who had it in him to become the man against time. That is to say, within him was born the power to become the one capable of interrupting with a process of complete rejuvenation the whole trend of decay of that time, thus interposing a new era within the life-and-death cycle of the ages.

Living later in Linz as a teenager, it was there—as vividly described by his boyhood friend, August Kubizek (*The Young Hitler I Knew*, 1954 Allan Wingate of London edition, Chapter VIII)—*"that in the course of a night of communion with the stars on the summit of the Freinberg, the heavens opened up to him the secret of his life, and Adolf Hitler came to know himself as a man against time. Thereafter, he was a person possessed by the driving force of destiny through access to the realm of higher perception; this showing in the extraordinary brilliance of his magnetic eyes and the extraordinary timbre of his compelling voice. By virtue of this power he was more than a man in ordinary form."*

So, it was that he was able miraculously to mobilise the discontent of a defeated nation under a degenerate democracy, moving a handful of men in Munich at the start to become through ever bigger meetings and membership and public support the power which took over the state, produced the earth shaking articulation of the national will at the Nuremberg rallies, embodied it in the most popular regime in all history, and nearly—very nearly indeed—gained the final goal of world supremacy essential for complete Aryan security.

Here is what stands out most is not that he failed at the final hurdle, but that he succeeded over so many for so long and so far, his being an achievement never before or after equalled.

Vastly exceeding any mere politician, Hitler was also of the nature of a seer and a priest, and an artist as well, whose supreme artistry was the pursuit of super humanity as the only surety of a postponement of time's work of decay.

Superhumanity was his ultimate ideal, because any really better society depends most of all not on better schemes but on better people to implement them; and producing better people depends most of all not on education and training, however important their roles, but on breeding them. The key to maximum progress is as simple as this. What is startling is man's failure, apart from National Socialism, to make use of it, thus is identified the exclusive and superlative merit of our creed.

Hitler sought superhumanity in two ways. Firstly, his concern was the protection of the Aryan as the human being of highest potentiality. His way to this was to make citizenship of the state a matter of membership of the nation, and membership of the nation a matter not of mere residence and thus mere geography but of race, and thus blood membership in the folk-community of the Aryan.

Secondly, within the Aryan folk-community his concern was the practice of positive eugenics to increase the best of the breed, decrease the lesser, and eliminate the defective worst. Here we have the pith and kernel of Hitler's message of salvation, the quintessence of the saviour's creed of National Socialism, his supreme justification, proof against all censure.

Vengeful time in the form of the forces of ruin allowed the messiah of the Aryans but six years of nominal peace barely to begin his great work of turning this decaying age into a golden one. The same span of years of war brought his death and the undoing of all he had done. Forty-four years later, has this wondrous man and his cause gone forever? Have they been completely defeated, utterly invalidated, and eternally relegated to the outer reaches of rejection as the acme of anathema?

Have the causes of the Untermenschen, the dark creeds of the "underdog," finally and forever ousted the Weltanschauung for an Atlantis of the sons of sunlight?

Indeed, it can well look so, at least at first glance and on the surface. Maybe, even on deeper consideration, his was indeed the last chance for a renaissance before the cyclic conclusion of this age by atomic cataclysm, environmental exhaustion, and the disintegration of a mongrelised mankind. Maybe, this will be the end not merely of an age but of the world itself, to be succeeded by life on another planet. Time—and the extent to which the saviour lives on in his followers—will tell!

Whatever the answer, one thing is certain: that is that "death" for a man of his magnitude can be no total extinction, as long as there are men alive to tell the tale. Instead, it is best restricted to a transition whereby the optical and aural image of the man passes entirely to the screen of memory. The counterfeit Christ of the Christians has remained "alive" through 2,000 years, becoming, on this plane of existence, something not lesser but far greater than his prototype in one of the many Jewish messiahs of the period. It can surely be similar for Adolf Hitler, the messiah of the Aryans.

Decisive for his transfiguration is the fact—never to be neglected—that he was beaten not morally but only materially, and this by a vastly greater muster of men and armaments, and after a resistance the magnificence of which the world had never before seen. The crucifixion of his creed was by the baleful spears of war alone, devoid of higher sanction from any worthier creed. His was the spiritual victory.

Thus, his military defeat at the hands of his spiritual inferiors, and all their denigration of him, can but serve to enhance his true image, assuring that he remains not only powerfully alive in spirit, but so much so that he can become the spiritual conqueror of the future.

In this reasoning is encapsulated the whole higher meaning of human life, which is the struggle of the spirit to its victory over matter. His enemies have no doubt of his power of resurrection, given the patient and imaginative toil of his true disciples for whom honour is loyalty.

His mountain home, the Berghof, had to be bombed to ruins, and then the ruins had to be blasted to smithereens lest the bare stones become a shrine, and then a dense plantation had to be grown over the bare site, lest the mere ground became a place of pilgrimage.

In that homeland of his, the democracy of the military conquerors had to concede moral defeat by dictating the perpetual banning of not only any revival of the NSDAP, but even the songs, the signs, and the ideas of his National Socialism.

Over all his enemies, even two score and four years after they have pronounced him dead—and prompting their never-ending daily defamation—hovers the haunting spectacle of a Hitler whose power defies death, and whose spirit lives on threatening their future.

Theirs is a dying world anyhow, spiritually stricken beyond hope of redemption, and thus incapable of averting cyclic demise. In their frantic fear of Hitler's spirit, they are well on the way to overreaching themselves through a denigration exceeding the bounds of credibility even for the captive herds of their media; thus causing a reaction in his favour. Nemesis may not only be possible, but not too far distant, they fear, and we hope. Some appreciable catalyst for this disillusionment can well come from the worldwide commemoration of his centenary, when—to the most agonizing disquiet of his enemies—we hold up the defiant torch to his memory with a thunderous affirmation that, despite all they have said and done, for us Hitler was right.

This centenary is indeed for us a high time of meditation, a veritable sacrament of our faith in National Socialism which always has been in the depth of its nature a political religion, and now must have this quality brought to the surface and spread throughout its substance in order to have the capacity to contest and conquer in the future.

As we focus our thoughts on the founder of our faith, embracing his spirit, we bring to life in memory all those who have lived and died in his cause, holding hands with them, and likewise with all those today, wherever they are, who actively serve that cause. Thus, we create in comradeship of spirit a bridge of dedication, past to present and present to future.

In so doing, there comes to us in consequence an emission of the sacred flame which imbued him. Then, in that moment is born within us an invincible renewal of the will to win. ***Heil Hitler!***

ADOLF HITLER: MAN, OF THE CENTURY

Fifty-two Easters ago I sat by that great river, the Rhine, a boy of 14 staying on holiday with a German family in the Hohenzollern Ringstrasse in Cologne. I went there from a much different England from that of today: an England where you could speak and write your mind on the Jewish issue free from race relations prohibition; where a coloured face was an oddity; where old ladies could go out at dark without being mugged; where the noxious noise known as 'pop" was non-existent; and where jeans were only workmen's overalls and not the daily dress of a decayed and disintegrating society.

I went to a Germany veritably reborn from the degradation of Weimar democracy, the nation electrified with an exultant feeling of corporate purpose and achievement which made every day a holiday, indeed literally a holy day, and this more than anything else because of the vision and the will of one marvel of a man in arousing millions in active service for the Aryan cause.

Never before or since in all history has any man tremendously championed the cause of our race as he whose centenary of birth falls on April 20th of this year, 1989. It is in this respect—transcending all comparative minutiae of criticism-that Adolf Hitler was then and is now to be hailed as a hero, and signified as right.

It was, of course, a certainty from the start that the whole assortment of anti-Aryan forces everywhere would congregate and contrive for his destruction: that was the very measure of his greatness. Poland, in the purblind protagonist of self-benefiting iniquities of the Versailles Treaty, provided a fulcrum for their foul purpose. Thus, it was that 1939 presented the last opportunity for all those outside Germany devoted to Aryan interests to rise up and stop the demented drive to disaster, reform their own countries, abandon the fratricidal nationalisms benefiting the common enemy, and bring about instead a unity of the Aryan peoples to withstand the multiplying numbers and mounting power of non-Aryans of this globe.

Sadly, they failed to do so, and so the most terrible of the blood-baths of the brothers followed with the most awful spectacle of so many Aryan nationalists aligning themselves with their real enemy, the anti-Aryan elements in their midst, and even today purporting to be proud of their war service against their ideological and racial kin.

I say this not from some smug standpoint of detached hindsight, but as one who, in his everlasting and agonizing reflection on the immensity of the Aryan catastrophe of 1939-45, derives some slight consolation from the fact that at the time, after a mere period of unsuccessful training in the Fleet Air Arm, he came to see the folly of the war, and accordingly, on political grounds, refused to fight against National Socialist Germany.

Only an overwhelming advantage of men and material enabled the powers of darkness to gain victory, and that victory was automatically the defeat of everything Aryan and the triumph of all things else. From the war and its ghastly conclusion have followed all our present afflictions and perils. This—the appalling state of Britain today—exemplifies what it was all about. This is what Britain's democrats fought for.

Sometime after the culminating disaster of 1945, I sat again in Germany, spending half a night on the debris of the "Berghof," the mountain home of the man of the century whose centenary currently occurs, and which Jewry's Allies first bombed and then, fearful even of the ruins, blasted them to smithereens. Amid the magic of the place, seemingly invested that night with his immortal spirit, and with the little, fairy-like lights of Berchtesgaden far below—as he
himself saw them so many times—and matched by the other little lights of the stars far above, one of which chose that time to depart its station and cascade across the firmament; I contemplated at length the immensity of what had been lost to us and the corresponding immensity of the price to be paid in the future.

This filled me anew with an intensity of certainty and his rightness, and so in a later year I returned to spend another night testifying to that certainty with a huge "Hitler was right!" slogan painted all over the one remaining boundary wall of the site.

As the centenary draws near and arrives, it is fitting that we contemplate the Britain, the Europe, and the world which would have been ours today, if this crazy country of ours had not in 1939 taken upon herself the role of a principal in the devastation of what was then the present to the despoilment of what is now our future, and had instead responded favourably to the message and the example of he who truly came as the saviour of our age.

Our towns today, instead of resounding to the twilight of the hordes from Africa and Asia, would still be the exclusive property of the descendants of their Anglo-Saxon and Celtic creators. Our youth, instead of being stricken with drugs and all the other debasements of the hideous "pop culture,' would be trekking in their physical splendour our byways and hills, adjoining with the kindred youth of other parts of Europe in great demonstrations of comradeship and confidence in the even greater glories of tomorrow on the road to superhumanity.

Our media, instead of being in all senses an alien instrument of corruption, ceaselessly promoting national decline and racial degeneration, would be consecrated to the upliftment of our people.

Our teachers, instead of being almost entirely sickly purveyors of pollution, would be salubrious models and guides for a just and orderly and prosperous folk-community.

Such contemplation is not simply some sterile projection of nostalgia but the purposeful source of that most powerful propellant for action which is a flaming fury.

It may well be, realistically, that we have had and lost our last chance to achieve such ideals, at least for the present age, and thus are now getting not nearer to but further away from the millennium. Even so, be sure that this is no cause whatever for surrender and inaction.

Resistance to evil is not an option but a never-ending bodily necessity for any and every real National Socialist, bringing a triumph of the will over any and all adversity, this being always a spiritual victory which is always the most important victory of all.

For April 20th, 1989, your passwords must therefore be: Never forget what the enemies of Hitler have done to your country! Never forgive them for what they have done! Never cease to strike back against them to the utmost that you can for what they have done! This is the only meaningful way to celebrate the day and to honour the man, making sure that those enemies will have good cause to remember and regret.

THE ENEMY WITHIN

On the centenary of his birth it needs to be noted that the cause of Adolf Hitler is confronted and conflicted not merely by the hostility of all the regular forces of the old order, but also and no less to its detriment by others who constitute one variety or another of an auxiliary enemy within. These comprise, firstly, the Strasserites: persons claiming to be nationalists or even National Socialists, but denigrating Hitler in tune with the champions of the old order, and upholding in his place the Strasser brothers, Otto and Gregor, and Ernst Rohm, whom Hitler had to eliminate from his party because of their treacherous disruption.

Secondly, there are those who, while plentifully making use of Hitler's name, are as plentifully harmful to his cause by their misunderstanding and misuse of it, and the consequent exploitation by the outer enemy of their association with it.

In this category we include the Hollywood Nazis: all those, in other words, who make use of National Socialism as nothing more than a political playtime devoted to its superficial trappings, thereby seeking to compensate for the deficiencies of their arrested development by dressing up, giving themselves titles, and performing sterile and egocentric antics.

Also, to be included are all those who, in their virtually total ignorance of what National Socialism really is, have not the slightest perception of, or respect for, the discipline, order and authority central to it, and who are simply excited to associate with it because of the enemy's distorted image of it as something violently notorious,
and who accordingly supply the enemy with living proof of validity of their distortion.

These latter are the dismal morons whose real cause is no more than crude hooliganism plentifully embellished with Swastikas and Iron Crosses and a flourish of Hitler salutes at football matches.

At this centenary let it be confirmed that there is no room in our ranks for such human rubbish. Likewise, let it be declared that National Socialism, so uniquely responsive to harmony and beauty, health and strength, has absolutely no room for "rock", that degenerate din of the African jungle to which the above hooligans, and also, others pretending to be National Socialists, are addicted, and which, we would have them know, Hitler would most certainly have prohibited. This is something that skinheads—if they are to elevate themselves from this category, have got to learn.

Returning to the Strasser brothers, they showed themselves to be more of the nature of national communists than true National Socialists, attacking private ownership of property (although upheld in the NSDAP's manifesto) in favour of mere possession on trust for the state (usufruct)—propounded by Otto Strasser in *The Structure of*

German Socialism (1931)—and acclaiming class warfare in the name of the proletariat. As early as 1925 Gregor Strasser in a speech in the Reichstag called for an "*economic revolution involving the nationalisation of the economy.*" On the 21st May, 1930, Otto Strasser met Hitler and demanded what he called "*real socialism*" and no attacks on Soviet Russia. Hitler replied: "*What you understand by socialism is nothing but Marxism.*"

The next day in continued discussion Otto Strasser demanded the nationalisation of industry, to which Hitler answered: "*Democracy has laid the world in ruins, and nevertheless you want to extend it to the economic sphere. It would be the end of the German economy.*" ("Who Financed Hitler", James & Suzanne Pool, Dial Press, New York, 1978; pp. 24 1-42)

If the Strassers had had their way, National Socialism would have never got to power, for they would have disrupted its appeal, frightening off essential support. No sensible person will really credit these men with the ability to succeed in Hitler's place in winning and holding the hearts of a nation. Both the Strassers were confined in their concern to the economic side of the cause to the disregard of other aspects such as the racial. This deficiency, aggravated by their distortion of the Party's economic policy, meant that they were always a couple of cuckoos in the nest.

National Socialism, properly understood, has never been a mere combination of conventional socialism spiced with nationalism, and thus yet another merely materialist doctrine.

It most certainly derives from its conception of the Folk a strong belief that this racial kinship justifies and decrees radical social justice, and thus the belief-, increased by its belief in the Leadership Principle, again derived from its racial belief—that private ownership and private enterprise must be subject to national regulation and supervision to ensure that its productive efficacy is fairly distributed and in accordance with national requirements; but it has never accepted the idea that nationalisation of property is the only and necessary means to adequate social justice, any more than it has been prepared to tolerate the anarchic inequity of liberal capitalism as the only answer and necessary means of preserving private property and enterprise.

It has always stood for reconciliation, not a conflict of private and corporate interests. However, along with this economic outlook, National Socialism has always been far more than this, being first and foremost a racial outlook from which its economic outlook has followed.

Otto Strasser left the NSDAP in 1930, setting himself up in opposition to Hitler. In 1931 he was behind the SA mutiny in Berlin—where many SA men were former communists—led by the Berlin SA chief, Captain Walter Stennes, who was advised and encouraged in the revolt by Otto Strasser. The authors James & Suzanne Pool, in their book earlier referred to, reach the conclusion (p. 378) that "the evidence indicates that Stennes was financed by several important industrialists who were intent on destroying the Nazis."

Otto Strasser himself admits in his book "*Flight from Terror*" that the foremost financial backer of Stennes was the Jewish multi- millionaire, steel and coal industrialist Otto Wolff.

Money also came from the major industrialist Hermann Bücher. Hitler, by personal intervention on the spot, quickly swung the great bulk of the SA men away from Stennes and Strasser.

On Hitler's attainment of power in 1933, Otto Strasser went first to Austria to continue his anti-Hitler campaign, then to Czechoslovakia. The Jew, Fritz Max Cahen, head of the German Resistance Movement against Hitler, describes in his book *Men Against Hitler (*Jarrolds, London, pp. 140-42), how, when he was in Prague in 1935, he had a conference with Otto Strasser and others leading to a plan for united opposition to Hitler, and how thereafter her met Strasser at least once a week.

The periodical *World Jewry* (28th August, 1936) carried the following report from its Prague correspondent: "The well- known rival of Herr Hitler, Otto Strasser. . . has published an appeal to the German Jewish emigrants to join the newly-formed organisation of German Jews headed by Herr Rossheim." . . . "In his opinion, the solution of the problem of the Jews in Germany lies in the direction of assimilation. . ."

In 1938 Otto Strasser moved to Switzerland, and afterwards to France. The British ambassador in Berlin, in a letter to the British Foreign Secretary on the 18th July 1939, said, "So many people, such as Otto Strasser and others of this world are seeking with intense pertinacity to drive us to war with Germany."

According to W.J. West in The Truth Betrayed (Duckworth, London, 1987), at the time of the Burgerbraukeller bomb plot, November 1939, which failed to kill Hitler as intended—and which the German authorities held to have been masterminded by the British Secret Service working through Otto Strasser-there were in fact very strong links between Strasser and the British authorities through Sir Robert Vansittart (Permanent Head of the Foreign Office and later Chief Diplomatic Advisor to the Government) who in October 1939 recommended to the Foreign Secretary Otto Strasser and Hermann Rauschning (another defector responsible for a volume of lies entitled "*Hitler Speaks*", exposed by Swiss historian Wolfgang Haenel). After the failure of the bomb plot it is significant that Vansittart turned against Strasser, clearly implying that his reputation was bound up with it (W.J West, p. 155).

Otto Strasser's friend and supporter, the author Douglas Reed, describes in the "*Prisoner of Ottawa*", (Jonathan Cape, London, 1953 pp. 172-75) how the former, while in France during the earlier part of the war, plotted against Germany with the Jew Georges Mandel, then Minister of the Interior in the Reynaud Government. With the fall of France, the roving traitor moved to Portugal from whence in 1940 the British helped him to reach Canada to continue his dirty work there.

Material from Otto Strasser went to make up the book Der Führer which was issued in the name of "Konrad Heiden", which, along with Rauschning's above-mentioned collection of lies, was used in formulating the indictment of the International Military Tribunal at Nuremberg whereby leading Germans were put to death and barbarously so by slow strangulation.

Strasser material was also made much use of by Dr. William C. Langer as acknowledged in his book *The Mind of Adolf Hitler* (Seeker & Warburg, London, 1972), a piece of wartime propaganda he was assigned to concoct by the American dirty tricks department known as the OSS.

The kind of help muck-spreader Strasser gave to Langer can be distinguished from Strasser's own offering of ordure entitled "*The Gangsters Around Hitler*" (W.H. Allen, London, undated but on British bookstalls in the middle of the war). Typical of its filth is his tale of a film made, he claims, of two titled ladies from the War Office executed for espionage: ". . . *when Hitler is unable to sleep he orders this film to be shown again and again, as he sits alone in the cellar which houses his private cinema*" (p. 43). Otto Strasser died in obscurity in Munich in 1974.

His brother Gregor stayed on in Hitler's party till 1932 when his disruptive intrigues came to a head. Authors James & Suzanne Pool, in "*Who Financed Hitler*" (p. 382), reveal that during the autumn of that year the Jew Paul Silverberg, a very wealthy industrialist, secretly gave money to Gregor Strasser who, like his brother, while presenting himself as such a strict opponent of big business, was quite prepared to be on its payroll.

The Jewish industrialist Otto Wolff, whom we have come across as paymaster for the Otto Strasser-Walter Stennes plot in 1931, also extended his purse to Gregor in this following year. "*Like Silverberg, Wolff had contributed heavily to Strasser. . .*" (p. 454): When in December, 1932, General Kurt von Schleicher became Chancellor, he immediately offered the position of Vice-Chancellor to Gregor Strasser with whom he was conspiring as a move to disrupt Hitler's party. Thereupon Hitler denounced him as a traitor, and he had to resign from the Party. This was not, however, the end of his subversion. He was involved in the Rohm plot two years later, and executed for this.

Ernst Rohm, head of the SA in 1934, was akin to the Strassers in political outlook, wanting to pursue a further revolution in the military sphere by elevating the SA in place of the Army, just as the Strassers wanted to regiment industry through public ownership. If Rohm had had his way, the consequent upset to the country, when Hitler had only newly taken hold of it, would very likely have meant the downfall of National Socialism.

At that time the SA, two million strong, was—under a Rohm behaving with increasing grandeur—running out of Hitler's control. A loyal SA commander, Victor Lutze, brought to Rudolf Hess eye-witness accounts of Rohm's plans to overthrow Hitler and bring about a second revolution (*Hess: The Missing Years*, David Irving, Macmillan, London, 1987, p. 22).

Also, Hitler's personal pilot, Hans Baur, in his book "*Hitler at my Side*" (Eichler Publishing Corp., U.S.A., 1986, p. 79) records that Hitler told the author that the Italian Ambassador in Paris had learned that Rohm was planning an uprising, and had entered into negotiations with the French who had assured him they would not interfere, and that Rohm had already drawn up his entire lists for a new government.

The Italian ambassador had notified the German ambassador in France who had informed Hitler, who, after agonising deliberation, had to order the arrest and execution of Rohm and his leading conspirators, thereby by his prompt and necessarily radical action very rightly preventing the vastly greater bloodshed and turmoil of civil war.

The Strasserites of today, devotees of the treacherous Gregor and Otto and fellow traveller Ernst Rohm, accuse Hitler of becoming a tool of big business, and betraying his cause and his followers thereby. The crucial point in this connection is not whether Hitler accepted vitally needed money from big business or any other quarter, but whether in so doing he allowed any money from any source to pervert him from the cause he believed in and stood for, and the answer to this must on any sensible survey be an emphatic "no!" Hitler, whatever the hopes of contributors, was never for purchase, and always remained the master whatever the money.

A major authority on the subject of NSDAP funds is the book here repeatedly referred to: "*"Who Financed Hitler"*, by James & Suzanne Pool. In 1923 industrialist Fritz Thyssen apparently gave 100,000 gold marks to General Ludendorff who acted as a conduit for various organisations, and part of this may have reached the NSDAP.

Industrialist Ernst von Borsig apparently contributed to the NSDAP in its early years, but not much more than to conservative parties as well. Not till 1927 did Hitler win a further supporter among industrialists, Emil Kirdorf, who thereafter mustered some financial help from others.

Throughout the period of prosperity Hitler received relatively few donations from important businessmen" (p. 155). In 1928 Hess met Thyssen who arranged a loan. In the summer of 1931 the Ruhrlade (group of industrialists) gave the NSDAP on Thyssen's recommendation a small sum (p. 278). In 1931 it was reported that Deterding of Royal Dutch-Shell both gave and loaned large sums to Hitler.

In that same year Hitler spoke at The Industry Club of Dusseldorf and Thyssen is later supposed to have written that as a result of this contact a number of larger contributions were made to the NSDAP; "supposed", we here say, because as will be seen Thyssen's writings are distinctly suspect.

The Pools say there may have been enough inflow to finance the current election campaign, but no great flow (p. 355). They estimate contributions from industry to the NSDAP 1930-32 as totalling not more than 600,000 marks. They mention help from Cologne banker, Baron Kurt von Schroder, but only in the form of arranging for NSDAP bills to be underwritten, not actually paid, and their overall conclusion is that "the primary source of Party revenue was not big business" (p. 385).

Otto Dietrich, NSDAP Press Chief, in his revised 1955 memoirs, says of the 1931 Industry Club of Dusseldorf meeting that insignificant sums were collected at the door, and nothing great followed.

Henry Ashby Turner in *"German Big Business and the Rise of Hitler"* (Oxford University Press, New York, 1985), another major authority, debunks the notion of Hitler's dependency on big business sustained by such as the writings attributed to Thyssen, showing in fact how little big business had to do with Hitler's success, its contributions never being critical, and most NSDAP money coming from membership dues, interest-free loans, and the admission charges at meetings.

Peter Drucker, the economist, in *"The End of Economic Man"*(London, 1939), endorses this conclusion on page 105: "As far as the Nazi Party is concerned, there is good reason to believe that, at least three-quarters of its funds, even after 1930, came from the weekly dues. . . and from the entrance fees to the mass meetings..."

A markedly inferior source, although much favoured by and advertised by Britain's contemporary Strasserites, is *"Wall Street and the Rise of Hitler"* by Antony C. Sutton (Bloomfield Books, Sudbury, U.K, 1976).

Behind the gusto of its blatant partisanship, it shows itself distinctly thin even as simply a survey of big business contributions to Hitler's rise to power, and totally lacking in any proof that in accepting such contributions Hitler was in any way whatsoever corrupted and deflected from his course, without which there can be no culpability on his part, only good sense in gaining necessary finance without compromise.

The book *"I Paid Hitler"*, attributed to Fritz Thyssen, has been made much of by the anti-Hitler front, but in 1948 Thyssen denied authorship of the book, saying that it was the work of Emery Reves who published it without permission or payment. Reves—a Jew whose father was formerly Rabbitz—was a New York publisher running an anti-Hitler propaganda machine, who acted as literary agent for Winston Churchill, and was responsible for the fictitious book by Hermann Rauschning, *Hitler Speaks*, wherein Rauschning claims to have had more than a hundred private talks with Hitler in which the latter revealed the entirety of his views and plans including a world empire, whereas this liar in fact only met Hitler four or five times, never alone, and never at length.

Strasserites, along with their idiotic depiction of Hitler as the paid lackey of big business, also try to reinforce their smears with the equally idiotic tale that Hitler had Jewish ancestry.

In the case of author Douglas Reed, the addled supporter of the sordid Otto Strasser, the nonsense even stretched to the extent of suggesting that Hitler was some satanic agent with the role from the start of misleader and destroyer of patriotic forces.

The "*Hitler was Jewish*" canard comes in two main variations, so take your pick! One of them makes out that Hitler's father's mother was once a domestic servant in the household of Baron Rothschild of Vienna, and there seduced by him. The prime source for this is none other than the book "I Paid Hitler" which, as we have just seen, the Jew Reves wrote while falsely attributing it to Fritz Thyssen.

The other version is that the seducing was done by a Jew named Frankenberger in his household at Graz. This whopper is said to have come to us from high NS official, Hans Frank, in memoirs said to have been written while in the custody of the Allies shortly before they hanged him at Nuremberg at the end of the war, when they may well have (as in other cases) done a bit of hand-guiding before neck-stretching.

Colin Cross, in *"Adolf Hitler"* (Hodder & Stoughton, London, 1973), says that the Graz Hebrew congregation had no Frankenberger among its members at the relevant time (p. 18); and Joachim C. Fest, in *"Hitler"* (Weidenfeld & Nicolson, London, 1974), says, *'Recent researches have further shaken the credibility of his statement, so that the whole notion can scarcely stand serious investigation*" (p.15).

Yet the self-styled "political soldiers" of the Nutty Farce which the present National Front has become, who have never faced and are never likely to face and endure what vast legions of men and women in Germany in peace and in war did in support of Adolf Hitler as epitome of their ideals, continue to defecate their denigration of him as a fake inferior to themselves, whereby these midgets most of all succeed in exhibiting their own childish and odious charlatanry.

BOOK REVIEW:
BLOOD AND SOIL BY ANNA BRAMWELL

On the slopes of Buckeberg, southwest of Hannover, in the Germany of the mid- 1930s up to half-a-million peasants used to gather at festivals to celebrate their newly-brought material prosperity and social elevation, while elsewhere in Europe agricultural depression and contempt for the "yokel" prevailed.

The German contrast resulted from the central importance given in National Socialist ideology to the value in interaction of blood and soil: the relationship of man in his distinctions of kinship and race to the earth with its divisions of region and country, and the soil from which he springs by way of the food on which he depends and to which he ultimately returns in the cycle of life.

A prominent contributor to Germany's agrarian revival was Walther Darre, later to be maligned and arraigned by the victorious Allies as a "Nazi Criminal," and today to be deceitfully hailed by Britain's Strasserites as *"one of Hitler's most feared and hated enemies"* in a reference of theirs to a new biography by Anna Bramwell which is unusually fair for someone who is not a National Socialist.

Born in Argentina, Darre spent a year at a school in England after moving to ancestral Germany, and in the last country took up agricultural training after service in World War I, becoming a state agricultural representative. He entered Nordic racialist circles early on by way of becoming acquainted with the seminal writings of Hans Gunther in 1923. The fusion in him of agricultural and racial idealism inspired between 1925 and 1930, two books and 56 articles upholding the peasantry as the racial custodians of the good life, and the very life-source of a nation. Industrialisation, the capitalism which is its motive force, the urban proliferation which is its concomitant, the Christianity which accommodated it: this in all its consequences had become for Darre the ultimate enemy, responsible for the decline of the peasantry and thus the alienation and degeneration of the nation.

Therefore, not only had measures to be taken to improve the economic position of the peasantry by protecting it against the ravages of world capitalism, but a new governing class, a hereditary nobility, had to be drawn from the revivified men of mother earth, leading to the creation of a peasant state in which the nation became identical with the peasantry.

PARTY LATECOMER

Darre, although early immersed in such revolutionary ideas, was no "alter Kampfer" or old fighter in the party which emerged to champion radical racialism more than any other before or after. He did not join the NSDAP until 1930 when he was offered a post within it, which as his biographer points out, conveys the impression that he came to National Socialism not as a committed believer but as one seeking to make use of its political apparatus for the advancement of his own personal views.

Heading the successful infiltration of the peasant's unions at the time when Hitler's rise to power required the acquisition of rural support, Darre on the attainment of power in 1933 was rewarded by appointment as Minister of Food and Agriculture, and also National Peasant Leader.

Effective reforms followed quickly as in so many other fields of National Socialist activity. Within the year came the Hereditary Farm Law, whereby only farmers of German or similar stock who could prove descent back to 1800 could inherit the protected farms, and the establishment of an agricultural marketing corporation which cut out the burdensome middleman, fixing prices, controlling quality and later laying down quotas.

A back-to-the-land program was brought in which established new and viable peasant settlements. By such means so successful was the drive to procure greater productivity from a comprehensively stimulated peasantry that by 1938 Germany had reached 81% self-sufficiency in food.

By then, however, Darre's standing was in decline, and by 1942 he was replaced by his second-in-command, Herbert Backe. In 1945 he surrendered to the victors and the Americans subsequently put him on trial, finding him guilty in 1949 of atrocities and offenses against civilian populations on account of his involvement in the compulsory purchase of Jewish-owned farmland at decreed instead of market valuations; and the expropriation of Polish and Jewish farmers in Poland in the course of resettling Germans in areas formerly German.

He was also convicted of plunder and spoilation in occupied territories because of his involvement in wartime agricultural policy in Poland; and of being a member of an organisation which had been branded as criminal, namely the National Leadership Corps of the Third Reich, by virtue of having been a minister. Sentenced to seven years for all this wickedness, he was freed on appeal in 1950, and died three years later of liver failure.

DEFECTS OF A VISIONARY

Darre's eclipsing defect was that of tunnel vision. As his biographer puts it: "*At root, Darre was a one issue man...*" The focus of his attention was constricted to what in resultant detachment was seen to be convincingly essential, but which pursued in detachment from realities of context constituted a mistake. "*He sees at once aims which could only be reached in a century or in decades.*" While it is the distinguishing quality of the visionary to see far ahead, it is also the common downfall of the same to be so intent on doing so as not to perceive obstacles in his path over which he proceeds to stumble. At a time when the infant National Socialist State was confronted on all sides by enemies intent on its destruction, Darre was in fact going so far as to advocate the de-industrialisation of Germany, leaving the cities to decay in favour of a reconstructed countryside. It was precisely such proclivity to impracticality which understandably brought about his progressive relegation as a dreamer.

Goring, in his capacity as head of the Four-Year Plan for economic development, certainly came to take this view of him when, in wartime, Darre agitated for the immediate conversion of German agriculture to organic practices, meaning the total exclusion of artificial fertilizers, causing the former to remonstrate that such a drastic transformation would at least initially reduce the market deliveries it was his concern to keep up, and should therefore be left till after the war. He had similar cause for objection when Darre's plans for immediate peasant settlement in occupied Poland clashed with Goring's requirements for food production there.

WIDER INSIGHT WANTING

Darre, in the blindness accompanying his attenuated outlook, never perceived and never understood the full picture of factors at work in the contemporary situation, and thus looked upon such as the incorporation of Czechoslovakia and the move against Russia as aberrations of imperialism by Hitler, and thus a collusion with forces inimical to the development of his peasant state, failing to recognise them as impositions of necessity in the continental conflict of ideas and interests.

For him the mass importation of foreign agricultural labourers appeared not as a temporary necessity in a life or death struggle for National Socialist Germany, but as a gross betrayal of the German peasants. As Anna Bramwell sums it up: "*The whole dimension of the 'National Interest' seemed to escape him...*"

Himmler, he came to regard as a prime instrument of Hitler's deviation into imperialism at the expense of true racialism, a complaint which his biographer seconds by way of citing co-option to membership of the ᛋᛋ a departure from its principle of racial selection, a criticism which perhaps overlooks the extent to which this minor practice could be a recognition of the fact of achievement as a demonstration of racial quality.

She adds to this the contention that: "*Certainly the ᛋᛋ elite eventually became pan-European, losing even its national as well as its racial character,*" a reference to the Waffen-ᛋᛋ (distinct from the general ᛋᛋ) by 1944 had certainly become massively composed of non-German formations, but this for the great majority of them precisely because of a racial bond, clearly European if not specifically Nordic, and a belief in a creed reflecting it, transcended the divisions of nationality.

Even with the very few formations which were not of European stock, the highly selective recruitment may well be said to have been aimed at what amounted to a racial elite from among the non-European peoples concerned.

THE INDISPENSABLE ONE

With the Strasserites seeking to exploit Darre and his dissatisfactions to discount and denigrate Hitler—and this despite the fact that Darre despised Otto Strasser as an "*incipient Bolshevik*" (Bramwell) —it is well to record and to remember that, without Hitler it is at least doubtful that National Socialism would ever have gained power.

Darre, along with his tunnel vision, also suffered from problems of personality, namely a tender vanity, a lack of tack, an unsociable disposition, and an increasing tendency to melancholic hypersensitivity which led to entries in his diary between 1942 and 1944 being so vituperative as to induce his wife to destroy that whole section after his death in order to protect his reputation.

It is thus easy to appreciate why his subordinate, Herbert Backe, a man of proven administrative efficiency who put the wider concern of national politics above any particular ambition, and who was a steadfast admirer of Hitler's leadership, companionable and straightforward, came to be preferred and to replace him.

Nevertheless, recognition of Darre's distinct flaws should not cause us to disregard or diminish the great amount that was justifiable in his message, and which merits our most careful consideration today, even more so than in his time because the situation has that much worsened.

At the core of his thinking lay the invincible and eternal verity that the true welfare of a country requires the maintenance of a thriving native breed rooted in the soil.

After the war and right up to his death, Darre continued to write on themes at least subsidiary to this such as the menace of soil erosion and the cumulative dangers of artificial fertilizers, as he had done in earlier days, and by virtue of which he stands out as a leading pioneer of ecological protection long preceding the "Green" movement of today.

MURDER AT SPANDAU

Rudolf Hess, the Prisoner of Peace, was finally laid to rest in the family grave at Wunsiedel on the 17th March 1988. At a time then and now when a War Crimes Inquiry is being conducted in Britain, we specify as a war crime the retention of this peace envoy in custody in Britain from 1941-1945, and, derivatively so, his wrongful conviction by a tribunal of victors' vengeance at Nuremberg in 1945- 1946, and his consequent imprisonment in Spandau Prison in West Berlin from then till 1987; and, finally, his ultimate murder there in that year. For all this war criminality we principally accuse the deceitful and dishonourable government of the United Kingdom in its various composition throughout this time.

Prior to his flight to Britain, Rudolf Hess had been energetically engaged with Hitler's knowledge and approval in seeking to end the conflict between Britain and Germany which both of them heartily deplored. Peter Allen, in *"The Crown and the Swastika"* (Robert Hale, London, 1983), claims that Rudolf Hess secretly met the Duke of Windsor in Portugal on the 28th July 1940, immediately after the fall of France, and that the latter approved German peace proposals presented by Hess as Hitler's official representative.

The Duke was then tricked by the British government of warmonger Winston Churchill whose Minister of Information, Walter Monckton, flew to Lisbon, pretended that the British government was going to give serious consideration to the proposals, and on the strength of this persuaded the Duke to depart for a post in the Bahamas.

Manoeuvred out of the way in this manner, the Duke had been manoeuvred off the British throne several years earlier, not only because of Mrs. Simpson, but because he was pro-Hitler and wanted Anglo-German unity.

Hess's son, Wolf Rudiger Hess, in *"My Father Rudolf Hess"* (W.H.Allen, London, 1986; p. 158), records that Albrecht Haushofer, assigned to do so by Hitler and Hess, met representatives of influential British circles in Geneva in August 1940, indicated that Britain was willing to make peace, if Germany cancelled the 1939 pact with Russia.

Hitler was in principle prepared to do this, but wished to wait until the complicated situation in the Balkans was clearer. However, the Churchill government was merely concerned to isolate Germany and her into conflict with Russia so that Churchill could achieve his long-standing aim of an alliance with Stalin against Hitler, something he had proposed to the Russian ambassador in London back in July 1934 (I.M. Maisky, *Who Helped Hitler?* p. 55), and, according to J.F.C. Fuller in *"The Second*

38

World War", put forward on four occasions: March 1938, September 1938, 4th and May 19th 1939.

Hess's son relates that in the winter 1940/1941, Albrecht Haushofer had discussions in Madrid with the British ambassador, Sir Samuel Hoare, through the medium of the Swedish Legation in Madrid (p.80).

In January 1941 the Vice-President of the International Red Cross, Carl Jacob Burckhardt, received unofficial information from London that Britain was prepared to make peace, and on the 28th April 1941 Albrecht Haushofer went to Geneva to see Burckhardt on the orders of Hitler and Hess (p.70).

It was during this period that Rudolf Hess, having conceived the desperate measure of a personal flight to Britain, had on the 10th January and the 30th April 1941 —prepared but been prevented from setting off, before finally doing the 10th May 1941. Also, Albrecht Haushofer had in September 1940 written to the Duke of Hamilton (with whom he had been in touch since 1936), at the suggestion of Rudolf to explore the way for negotiations.

This letter fell into the hands of Britain's Secret Intelligence Service says David Irving in *"Churchill's War"*, Veritas, Australia, 1987; p. 650), according to Dr. Eduard Benes, ex-President of Czechoslovakia, the SIS saw the Haushofer approach as "*an excellent opportunity*", sent a reply purporting to be from Hamilton, and further letters arranged for Hess to fly to the Duke's estate.

As to Hitler's prior knowledge of Hess's flight on the 10th May 1941, according to Wulf Schwarzwaller (*Rudolf Hess*, Quartet, London, 1988; p. 156), Hess's former adjutant, Alfred Leitgen, remembers overhearing snatches of a conversation between Hitler and Hess in which there was mention of Albrecht Haushofer and Hamilton, no problems with the aeroplane, and (from Hess) of declaring him insane.

The first German radio communique concerning Hess's flight was not until the evening (20:00 hrs.) of the 12th May, suggesting that Hitler held his hand to see if Britain responded favourably to Hess's mission.

Thereafter, as could be the pre-arranged protection, when it was seen that the mission was unsuccessful, the German authorities stated that Hess had become unbalanced.

Hess's flight significantly occurred at a time when—contrary to the Allied picture of an unprovoked attack on Russia by Germany in late June of 1941 —Russia was preparing to make a surprise attack on Germany.

Ernst Topitsch, in *"Stalin's War"* (St. Martin's Press, New York, 1987), assembles evidence that by late summer, 1941, preparations for a mass offensive against Germany would have been concluded. On page 106, Major General Grigorenko is quoted as saying, "*More than half the troops of our Western Military Region were in the area round Bialystok to the West of that, that is in an area which projected into enemy territory. There could only be one reason for such a distribution, namely that these troops were intended for a surprise offensive.*"

In *"Truth for Germany"* (Verlag fur Volkstum und seitgeschichtsforschung, Viotho, West Germany; p. 411) Udo Walendy quotes H.A. Jacobsen & H. Dollinger, *"The Second World War in Pictures and Documents"* (Vol. 1, p. 372) as stating that Russia concentrated in her western territories up to June 1941 13 armies with more than 131 infantry divisions, 23 cavalry divisions, 36 motorized brigades and about 40 tank divisions with almost 4.7 million soldiers. Walendy (p. 416) also cites H.G Seraphim's *"The German-Russian Relations 1939—1941"* (p. 85) that Russian General Vlassov stated in 1942 in Berlin after his capture, "*The attack was intended for August/September 1941.*"

Victor Suvorov, a former member of the Soviet General Staff, in an article in The Journal of the Royal United Services Institute for Defense Studies (London; June 1985), assembled very detailed information to show that beginning in March, 1941, and assuming a huge scale in May and June, Soviet troops were being moved to and concentrated on the German border in preparation for a Soviet attack on Germany.

"*If Hitler had not attacked first, Stalin would have had 23 armies and more than 20 independent corps facing him. This took place before general mobilisation.*" Suvorov shows that the measures were clearly offensive, not defensive.

"*It seems certain that the Soviet concentration on the frontier was due to be completed by 10 July. Thus, the German blow which fell just 19 days earlier found the Red Army in a most unfavourable situation—in railway wagons.*"

German intelligence certainly learned what was going on, this causing Hitler to consider a pre-emptive strike a necessity, and he set in motion preparations for this at the end of April, 1941, just before Hess's flight. However, he only confirmed the final forward movement a month in advance, that is to say, after it had become clear that Hess's mission had been unsuccessful; and both events shortly followed a Kremlin banquet on the 5th May at which Stalin announced in a supposedly secret speech—which German agents are said to have reported to Hitler almost at once—"*Our war plan is ready.... It follows that over the next two months we can begin the fight with Germany.*" (Hitler 's War, David Irving, Viking Press, U.S.A.;1977; pp. 238 & 239.)

Attempting to put together and interpret the items of information here presented so as to form a full picture of Hess's flight, it seems evident that the flight was no self-contained impulse of purely personal initiative as is the common conception. It came after a long period of attempted negotiation to which Hitler was fully a party, and was most likely made with his approval. It came, furthermore, almost certainly in response to encouraging intimations from the British authorities, in part at least making use of the Duke of Hamilton, and amounting to giving the go-ahead green light; but all this on their part as merely a ruse to lure Hess to Britain, and this as part of Churchill's design to bring Stalin into the war in alliance with Britain against Germany.

In this design Hess was conceived as the catalyst. Stalin for his part had made a pact with Hitler to encourage Hitler to confront the West. Now, in the ensuing war, hopes by Germany of an arrangement with Britain could both encourage Hitler to feel it opportune to fight Russia and, in turn, encourage Russia to feel it had to forestall such an attack, even though it would be far more to her advantage to attack a Germany still at war with the West. This assuredly is the key to the mystery.

Hess is likely to have brought over extensive peace proposals which have been hidden from the British public along with other aspects of his flight just discussed. His proposals were of course ignored, and he was kept in close custody ever afterwards in order to prevent his disclosure of the full background to his flight, his peace proposals, and his treatment in custody.

This happened despite the fact that Hess appears to have been in a position of a bearer of a Flag of Truce under Article 32 of the Hague Convention. This piece of international law protects such a person from being held as a prisoner of war, or put under any other form of confinement after negotiations. Churchill, it is to be noted in this connection, put Hess under the responsibility of the War Ministry as if in the category of a prisoner of war, instead of the Home Office, as would befit the bearer of a Flag of Truce.

Repeated reference has been made to the part played by Albrecht Haushofer. David Irving, in *"Rudolf Hess: The Missing Years 1941-45"* (Macmillan, London,1987; p. 57), states that he had pre-war contact in London with the Special Intelligence Service.

Early in 1940 he was introduced into the Wednesday Society, a Centre of German resistance to Hitler, says Hess's son on p. 72 of his book. He was arrested in 1944 on suspicion of being involved in the July plot to murder Hitler and seize power; and he was shot just before the end of the war.

Much has been made of Hess's alleged "abnormality" and "instability" during his imprisonment in Britain from the time of his arrival till, four years later, his transfer to Germany for trial. This portrayal was undoubtedly deceitfully done by the British authorities in order to discredit Hess and thereby his peace flight at a time when Churchill was fearful of the potential response in the country menacing his position. It stopped just short of declaring him positively insane, since this condition would have entitled him as a prisoner of war to repatriation under the Geneva Convention.

The "*abnormality*" and "*instability*", where they were not a matter of a mere loss of memory which Hess feigned in order to protect his knowledge of confidential German matters under intensive questioning, was due to the wrongful and oppressive conditions to which he was subjected.

Although the Geneva Convention prohibited electronic eavesdropping on prisoners of war, apparatus was installed at Mytchett Place at Aldershot before he arrived (D. Irving, Rudolf Hess; p. 101). Military Intelligence 6 provided "*companions*" for Hess, including Zionist sympathizer, Major Frank E. Foley (p. 103),
with the job of penetrating Hess's mind, and seemingly drugs were used to this end (p. 107). Hence Hess's repeated protests and recurrent fear that he was being "poisoned" which his captors paraded as proof of his unsoundness of mind.

Hess was put in the hands of a Jewish psychiatrist, RAMC Major R.V. Dicks who worked with MI6 (SIS), and who posed as a regular doctor, and who progressed to portraying Hess as of unsound mind. Dicks was by then the author of a new textbook, "*Analysis under Hypnotics*", and he is known to have eventually injected Hess with the narcotic Evipan. (For these preceding facts, see Irving on Hess.) It has elsewhere been reported that documents in the U.S.A. indicated that behavioural peculiarities in Hess were caused by the administration of "*truth drugs*". The British Foreign Office significantly refused a request by Hess's wife that the International Red Cross be allowed to examine her husband.

Moved to Nuremberg in 1945, one of the panels appointed to pronounce on his fitness to stand trial there was a Prof. Ewen Cameron. This worthy was sponsored by the American Central Intelligence Agency to research brainwashing when he ran the Allan Memorial Institute in Montreal from 1943 to 1967. While doing so it was alleged that, for one example, one patient was injected with LSD, put to sleep for up to 50 days at a time, given repeated electric shocks, made to wear a helmet with speakers through which instructions were endlessly conveyed to him; and ended up a physical and mental wreck. (Daily Telegraph London, 12th September 1988.) Just imagine this had been a German in Hitler's days, and what the Simon Wiesenthal Centre would have made of it now—and all the British media!

Hess's continued incarceration from then till his death in 1987—41 years of his total caging for a monstrous 46 years—was arranged in order to exact the utmost in victors' vengeance while, fully as importantly, gagging him from making known the truth about his flight which would have been most damaging to the British government.

The means to this end was the International Military Tribunal at Nuremberg, a creation of, by and for the victors regardless of real justice which it most flagrantly disregarded. For instance, Article 3 of its Charter disallowed objections that the judges, being nominated by the victors, were prejudiced. Article 6 allowed accusations only against representatives of the Axis Powers. Article 19 laid down that the Tribunal should not be bound by the technical rules of evidence.

Article 21 provided that proof was not required for what the prosecutors regarded as facts generally known. Britain's Judge G. Lawrence refused to allow Hess's counsel to discuss the Treaty of Versailles, even though the Prosecution had introduced the subject by arguing that the struggle for its revision had been a long-planned conspiracy against peace.

One of the American judges at Nuremberg, Francis Biddle, later revealed in the American Heritage journal, Vol. XIII, No. 5, August 1962, that the U.S. judges knowingly permitted the Soviet prosecutor to admit false evidence against the defendants. Hess was convicted—with the rich irony of a Russian judge reading out the findings against him—of "Crimes Against Peace" encompassing the following: —He had urged the importance of armaments, given support to military preparations, and signed the decree introducing conscription. He had been in Vienna when the German troops entered the city, and had signed the law for the union of Germany and Austria, having earlier made speeches in favour of this.

He had co-operated with the Sudeten National Socialists and after the incorporation of the Sudetenland in the Reich he had carried out the fusion of their party with the NSDAP.

In June, 1939, he had been authorised to participate in the administration of both Austria and the Sudetenland, and in August, 1939, he had given public approval to Hitler's policy concerning Poland, and was a party to taking over Danzig and certain areas in Poland. As Hitler's close confidant he must have known of and thus be responsible for Hitler's "*plans of aggression*". (See Irving on Hess.)

For this— comparable to what Western politicians have regularly done, and never been charged or punished for—the man who tried to make peace was convicted of violating peace, and sentenced to life imprisonment.

Sent to Spandau Prison in West Berlin, conditions there were so bad that Pastor Casalis, a chaplain at the prison, said in November, 1948, that the prisoners were dying slowly of starvation. "*Spandau,*" he said, "*has become a place of mental torture . . .*" He spoke of "*an atmosphere of refined sadism.*"

Even when conditions later improved, Hess continued to be subjected to such harshly punitive restrictions as never to be allowed to touch his wife or son or grandchildren, and for over half of his total of 46 years behind bars he suffered the additional hardship of solitary confinement. Nevertheless, despite nearly half a century of such veritable torture, and despite the unsuccessful efforts of a French chaplain to get him to sign a declaration of remorse this Pastor Gabel had himself composed, he remained steadfast in his National Socialist beliefs and in his loyalty to and esteem for his friend and leader, Adolf Hitler. His martyred life ended on the afternoon of August 17th, 1987.

A succession of conflicting announcements as to where and how he died followed from the Allied authorities, exciting profound suspicion. Although the Americans were at the time in rotational charge of Spandau, the British insisted that the death be investigated solely by the Special Investigation Branch of the British Military Police, and that the post mortem be conducted by a British Army pathologist. This autopsy, performed two days later by Prof. James Cameron, indicated that death was due to suicide by hanging, but the Russians refused to countersign the verdict. At it, and not before and during the investigations by the Military Police, an alleged suicide note was discovered in the clothing of the corpse which, when he eventually obtained it, Hess's son saw to be highly suspect, being scrawled on the back of an old letter from the son's wife which lacked the usual prison stamp, and being without signs of having been in the pocket of a body very roughly handled in ostensible efforts at resuscitation which caused nine ribs and the breastbone to be broken, and the stomach to be blown up like a balloon because a tube for oxygen was wrongly inserted in the esophagus instead of the windpipe. The piece of electric flex with which he was supposed to have hanged himself had been wiped clean with acetone by the time the Military Police investigating team arrived, and the British Military Governor of Spandau, Lt- Col. A.H. Le Tissier later told the son's wife that he had destroyed it.

A second autopsy, arranged by Hess's family and conducted by Prof. W. Spann of Munich University found marks around Hess's neck and throat which indicated he was throttled not hanged, while his hands showed he had not wound the flex round a hand to exert the necessary pressure on his neck for self-strangulation; the inescapable implication being that he had been murdered.

In support of this conclusion this second autopsy showed that the victim suffered from disabilities which virtually rendered him incapable of hanging himself—or, for that matter, strangling himself. According to various sources, including this second autopsy, Rudolf Hess so suffered from advanced arthritis and curvature of the spine—his left arm being of little use because of a frozen shoulder which prevented it being lifted above the horizontal in front and not even as high as that out to the side, his head being incapable of raising backwards to enable him to look up or of turning more than a few degrees to the left and halfway to the right—that he could never have reached above his head to tie a noose.

Furthermore, the muscles of the hands of this 93 -year-old man was so weak that he had trouble gripping anything, and thus it was impossible for him to tie a knot to hang himself, or to apply the pressure necessary for self- strangulation (when in any event unconsciousness and consequent relaxation of the grip precedes and prevents death). Some other person or persons therefore killed him: that must be our verdict.

Whom could they be acting for? Was it the Russians whom Britain has always blamed for Hess's continued imprisonment? The Russians, despite their fulminations against Hess on occasions, were on other occasions prepared to make use of him.

The German historian, Dr. Werner Maser, has asserted that back in 1952, on the night of March 17th, when the Russians were in charge of the prison, they took Hess to East Germany to a meeting with Kremlin officials at which Otto Grotewohl, the East German Prime Minister and Maser's source of information, was present. There Hess was offered immediate freedom, if he would head a new party to reconcile former National Socialists to communist rule. Hess refused, and was returned to prison for 35 more years.

In April 1987, four months before his father's murder, Wolf Ruediger Hess was amazed to find that his approaches to the Russians suddenly had a favourable response. He was summoned to the Soviet Consulate in West Berlin where officials hinted that his father's imprisonment might soon end.

Also, on June 21st, 1987, in a reply to a listener in Germany, Radio Moscow (Department of German language broadcasts) wrote: "*Recent remarks by the head of our government, Mikhail Gorbachev, permit the expression of hope that your long-time efforts in behalf of the release of war criminal Rudolf Hess may soon be crowned by success.*"

It seems that Gorbachev did intend to release Hess unilaterally during a Soviet turn of administration at Spandau as a powerful propaganda stroke to exhibit to a nicety the kind tendencies of a reformed Soviet regime, even towards a notorious old enemy it had formerly fiercely denounced.

The Russians let the West German President know of their intention. He tipped of the British who expressed through him a resolute refusal to accept this.

The possibility of Hess's release now put the British in a panic. Hitherto they had been able to rely on the Russian refusal to agree to Hess's release as the means of keeping him and his secrets locked up forever, while they, in characteristically hypocritical style, posed as the forgiving ones favouring his release. What then is said to have happened according to information from American personnel at Spandau reaching German friends of theirs is as follows.

In an operation carried out in great haste to proceed even any advance announcement of Gorbachev's intention, let alone its implementation, and thus accounting for flaws, two British Special Air Service men were put into the prison to kill Hess, and the American, French and Israeli secret services were acquainted beforehand, but not the Russian and West German.

These two assassins were spotted beforehand on the afternoon in question in the vicinity of the garden shed where Hess met his death.

In the region of 3:15 to 3:30, the American warder on duty to accompany Hess on his daily visit to the garden and there to the garden shed, was by a curious coincidence called away to answer a telephone call in the main cell block, leaving Hess in the garden shed.

During his absence the SAS men evidently attacked the old man who, despite his great age and great disabilities, put up a fight and these fiends tried to throttle him with flex, and then make it look like suicide. However, although rendered unconscious, the old man was still alive when the warder returned and summoned help. The U.S. officer in charge of the guard, seemingly a party to the assassination, called a British military ambulance which took Hess away, accompanied by the two SAS men who were seen getting into it. Hess then "died" on the way to the hospital. (Probably with further assistance from the assassins-our note.)

The guilty ones were well-protected from justice by the provisions of their masters. No public inquest, as normal under British law, was held because Hess, although in custody in the British sector of Berlin, was a prisoner of the four Allies, and any process concerning them on German soil requires the express permission of the Allied power or powers involved.

The West Berlin state prosecutor, "*following information received from numerous sources,*" initiated an enquiry into Hess's death in February 1988, but it was suspended the following month (Independent, London, 18th March, 1988).

The Chairman of the British Bar's European group commented at the time of Hess's death that Rudolf Hess was incarcerated under a sentence imposed by an ad hoc tribunal with no legal status under any national law {Daily Telegraph, London, 20th August 1987).

Thus, his custody—and all that followed from it, including his death—became a matter beyond and thus above the normal law by virtue of the inter-governmental pact of the victors setting up the tribunal. Murder at Spandau was thus by higher decree permissible.

To complete the shrouding of the case of the corpse, already so well-attended to, the British government's Hess papers are placed beyond reach till 2017, and by then you can be sure that anything revealing will have conveniently disappeared.

Hugh Thomas, a former British Army surgeon assigned to Spandau, believes the prisoner was murdered, but also believes that he was not Rudolf Hess but a double sent by Himmler who had the real man murdered in 1941.

Thomas's case principally rests on his claim that the prisoner did not have the scars he should have had due to a wound in the First World War. As against this, it is a fact that scar tissue in such an old man could be difficult to detect.

Also, for what it is worth, Mrs. Lynda Chalker, Minister of State at the Foreign Office, was reported in "The Scotsman" (26th February 1988) as stating that the British government had concluded on the basis of various studies and the British post mortem that the man was indeed Hess.

Additionally, the "Sunday Times" (12th June 1988) reported that Charles A. Gabel, the French chaplain at Spandau, had, in a book of his published in Paris in 1988, revealed that after Thomas first published his theory in 1979, two allied doctors visited Hess and did with difficulty find the wound scars. If Thomas is to be believed—and if thus it is to be believed that Hess's wife and son have been deceived for decades as to the prisoner's identity—we are still left with the conundrum which Thomas never really comes to grips with: why would such an imposter as the prisoner still hide the truth decades after the war, and thus acquiesce in his imprisonment till death—when the insertion of deliberate anomalies in his letters to relatives of Hess could easily be made the means of communicating his imposture? The absence of any satisfactory answer to this must discredit Mr. Thomas's theory completely.

As the most recent important development in the case of Rudolf Hess's death, a witness who was at Spandau at the time has come forward to testify that it was murder. Tunisian-born Abdallah Melaouhi was the victim's nurse at Spandau for the last four years of his life, and thereby the closest person to him.

Interviewed on the Newsnight program of Britain's BBC Television Channel 2 on the 28th February 1989, Melaouhi had this to say, according to an official transcript in our possession: -When shortly before his death, there were reports that the Russians were relenting and Hess would be freed, "*Hess wasn't very happy about it. Hess said, 'Now something is going to happen to me.'* ... He told me "*Mr. Melaouhi, now they are going to kill me.*"

On the 17th August 1987, Melaouhi was at lunch in the canteen adjoining the prison when a telephone call from the French warder summoned him back urgently. He returned immediately to the prison and rang the bell. Usually he was admitted right away, but on that day, he had to wait for 15 minutes. When he was let in he found his way to the garden hut was blocked. Eventually he managed to get to it by a long way around, taking 40 minutes instead of four minutes the normal way.

He saw no cable around or anywhere near Hess's neck and the extension cable with which the authorities say Hess hanged himself was still in his normal place, one end connected to the lamp and the other in the wall socket.

"*His body was quite a distance away from the window where the TV claimed he hanged himself and the chair was in a totally different place from usual. I know the garden hut very well. The floor was covered with a straw mat but on that day, everything was upside down as if a wrestling match had taken place. The armchair where Mr. Hess always sat had flown about three-and-a-half meters across the room, the lamp had fallen over. It was as if someone had tried to kill him and he'd tried to save himself.*"

Melaouhi continued, "*There were three people there, a warder who has been working in Spandau for eight years and two American soldiers, well they were dressed in American uniforms...* (Our note: it would be hardly surprising if, in the circumstances of the American turn of duty, the SAS men had donned American uniforms with the connivance of the American authorities.) ... *I'd never seen soldiers near Hess before, and precisely on that day they were there.*"

He explained that soldiers were in Spandau to guard the prison, not the prisoner, which was strictly the job of the civilian warders. Said Melaouhi: "*Rudolf Hess was so weak he needed a special chair to help him to stand up. He walked bent over with a cane and was almost blind. If he ever fell to the ground, he couldn't get up again. His hands were crippled with arthritis. He couldn't tie his shoe laces, let alone lift his hands high enough to kill himself.*"

Newsnight stated that Scotland Yard had been looking into the case for a month, following a visit by Hess's son with evidence including a signed statement from Abdallah Melaouhi and the second autopsy report of Prof. Spann; but that so far there had been no attempt by the Metropolitan Police to contact either of these witnesses, and official sources close to the enquiry had said that "it is unlikely the case will be pursued." (For readers wishing to tackle the Metropolitan Police on this, the address is New Scotland Yard, Broadway, London, SW1.)

Rudolf Hess Gesellschaft, Postfach 1 122, D-8033 Planegg, West Germany, has now replaced the former society for the release of Rudolf Hess, and incorporates its former French counterpart.

It is an international association—President: Wolf Ruediger Hess—existing as a memorial to Rudolf Hess, and as such concerned with his work in Germany prior to

National Socialism: Vanguard of the Future

his flight to Britain, the flight itself, his subsequent captivity, and the manner of his death. Two publications are in course of preparation.

Gothic Ripples, whose editor has campaigned for Rudolf Hess for 40 years, proposed that henceforth May 10th each year be observed worldwide as RUDOLF HESS DAY in honour of this truly great and greatly harmed idealist.

It was late on this day in 1941 that he landed in a field near to Floors Farm Cottage, itself near to Floors Farm near to Eaglesham House, the exact spot being marked by a stone. The area is a little south of Glasgow in Scotland. The Ordnance Survey Landranger Map 64 shows the spot as grid reference OS 561 540. Visitors to the spot should secure permission from the Farm or its Cottage before going on to the ground, taking care not to spoil things for others by in any way unnecessarily antagonising the owner or occupant of the ground or other local people.

II: THE PRESENT: NATIONAL SOCIALISM TODAY

Colin Jordan does not consider National Socialism to be merely or even primarily a matter of historical interest or nostalgia— quite the contrary. In these two articles, written 15 years apart, he deals with National Socialism in a modern context.

"*'National Socialism: A Philosophical Appraisal* "first appeared as the lead article in the premier issue of "*"National Socialist World"*, an ideological journal published in the 1960s by the World Union of National Socialists.

In it, the author places National Socialism in its proper historic perspective as a movement of "*rebirth*" and "*renewal,"* centred around the Folk, or racial community, and which is characterised by *"thinking with the blood."*

'*National Socialism: World Creed for the Future*" originally appeared in the Winter, 1981, issue of the WUNS journal *"The National Socialist"*, under the title *'National Socialism: Our World Creed in the 1980s.*"

In this major essay, Jordan charts a course of strategic and ideological development for the Movement. Many consider this to be his most important work to date. – *Editor*

NATIONAL SOCIALISM: A PHILOSOPHICAL APPRAISAL

Twenty-one years after the physical defeat of National Socialist Germany in the outcome of her heroic struggle against the overwhelming array of men and materials marshalled against her by the Bolshevik-Democratic alliance, the appearance of this journal in 1966 reflects that revival of National Socialism which is the feature of the day.

That the creed should live on and manifest itself as it does now, after being subjected to two decades of the greatest campaign of vilification which the world has ever known, is a proof of its continuing validity and appeal and its worthiness for the future. It has survived the flames of war and the tempest of vilification because, when war has done its worst and vilification has run its entire gamut, National Socialism remains, in the final analysis, synonymous with higher man's will to survive, his instinct for health and strength, and his desire for beauty in life; and as long as that will, that instinct and that desire remain on this earth, National Socialism will remain indestructible.

Beyond and behind all the minutiae of political implementation and the particularities of time and place, National Socialism, properly understood, is nothing less than an orientation on the mind, the dominant impulse of which is to live life to the full, through the development of one's potentialities and the satisfaction of one's needs, under conditions of natural competition and selection, reconciled to cooperation, within the organized community of the folk.

In this its roots go back to Plato's Greece and his conception of a natural life, consisting in the full realisation of man's true nature through the conducive power of government within his native community.

It echoes the Roman notion of dutiful citizenship: the notion that the good and noble life consists in Stoic service to the state.

It revives the blood feelings and sense of community of the Nordic tribes of early Europe: the feeling that man is essentially a member of the folk, and that all members of the folk are bound together closely with reciprocal duties and obligations.

National Socialism, in this way, reaches back to the old, healthy, organic values of life in revolt against the whole structure of thought of liberalism and democracy, with its cash nexus; its excessive individualism; its view of man as a folkless, interchangeable unit of world population; its spiritual justification in a debased Christianity embracing a sickly "*humanitarianism*," which will always tolerate a greater harm for the sake of avoiding a lesser one; and its fraudulent contention that the artificially induced and numerically determined wishes of the mass are all-important criteria.

History is a saga of social decay and renewal. National Socialism is the 20th century's remedy of renewal for the great degeneration of modern times under the disintegrating, debasing, and emasculating thought and practice which emerged with the disruption of the old medieval order of stability by the developing forces of capitalism and the industrial revolution; flourished under the laissez-faire liberalism of the 18th and 19th centuries; came to a climax under the democracy of the 19th and 20th centuries; and will result in the world triumph of communism by the end of this 20th century unless National Socialism comes to power in time, and over a sufficient area of the globe.

National Socialism is therefore immensely more than a transitory political scheme. It is a historic tendency of rebirth: our age's movement of renaissance, a movement revolutionary in scope and spirit, seeking no compromise with the present order, its pernicious practices, and its false values, but their complete replacement.

As such it is worldwide and it is life-wide. It is worldwide in that, in its essentials, it is valid and vital universally, qualified only by the fact that it is Aryan in its emanation and tradition, and upholds and depends on the qualities that are to be found par excellence in the Aryan people. It is life-wide in that it is not an aspect of life, but the whole of life seen from one aspect. It is an attitude of mind expressible in respect of virtually anything and everything. National Socialism stands relentlessly opposed to every manifestation of ill-health, ugliness, and degeneracy in the cultural and spiritual, no less than in the economic and political spheres. In fact, it constitutes a way of life. A man does not call himself a National Socialist as a mere label of intellectual endorsement. He is born with a propensity to National Socialism, his mind aesthetically craving the discernment and the fulfilment of a healthy pattern of life, and he not only thinks and feels, but acts as a National Socialist, if he is really and entirely one.

Total in its scope and thought, National Socialism amounts to a philosophy and a faith. It evaluates good and bad, right and wrong, as that which benefits or harms the folk; and, in place of the sentimental debility of the democratic mind, accepts that the end justifies the means, providing the means do not contradict the end.

It sets a meaning and purpose of cosmic dimension to life as a personal fulfilment, within the continuity and development of the folk, between germination in the womb out of the bloodline of the folk, and the metamorphosis of the grave, with its physical redistribution to the universe.

The basic criterion and primary value of National Socialism, from which all else springs, is, as Adolf Hitler makes clear in Mein Kampf its concept of the folk, seen as man's essential environment and, indeed, his extension of personality.

The significance of the folk is, primarily, that of a racial community. It is the ethnical enlargement of the family. Man is not a self-contained unit and an end in himself, as the sages of liberalism and democracy assert. He belongs to his folk.

His life, as a part, is interwoven with the life of the whole, not only present, but past and future, for while men come and go the folk lives on, continuous, eternal, providing its members perform their duty to it. Thus, in identifying himself with his folk man prolongs himself through the multiplicity of his ancestors and his descendants, and thereby attains immortality.

The folk exists in smaller and larger forms, ranging from the family, to the clan, to the tribe or regional community, thence to the nation, and beyond to the race. In modern times, the conception of the folk has been too largely identified with the nations of the contemporary states.

The feeling of kinship and community, which rightly expanded from the tribe and petty kingdom to the modern nation-state, has, however, become far too concentrated at this level. The lower and smaller, but equally important, communities within the nation-state have been disrupted and deprived of vitality, while the expansion of folk consciousness from the level of the nation-state to that of the entire race has been checked.

Yet folk feeling, to be wholesomely potent, must flow from its roots through the local and provincial communities to the limits of the race, because the full security and prosperity of the parts can only be found in that of the whole.

Today and in the future National Socialism must embody this essential extension of the feeling of kinship and community beyond the bounds of the contemporary nation- state and conventional nationalism, so that the nation-state becomes an intermediate unit in the structure of the folk, and its nationalism and racialism become integrally subordinate to a nationalism of the whole race.

At the same time, the local communities require to be revived, the provincial sub-nations recognised and respected, and peoples subject to an undesired, alien rule given their ethnic freedom by separation.

National Socialism's belief in the folk, as a basic value, and its totality of outlook, result, figuratively speaking, in thinking with the blood on all questions.

This immediately and inevitably gives rise to the definition of citizenship as a matter of race: only those who are members of the folk are members of the nation, and only those who are members of the nation can be citizens of the state—to paraphrase the fourth of the Twenty-five Points of Adolf Hitler's NSDAP.

It also generates the belief that it is necessary not merely to preserve the racial character of the folk, but also, by eugenic measures, to improve the quality of the folk. It is National Socialism's revolutionary contention that the way of real progress lies in the breeding of better human beings.

Since all the citizens are of the same race, they have a transcendent bond of kinship uniting them as blood brothers above all sectional and class differences and personal distinctions. National unity, i.e., cohesion and corporate life in place of the class warfare of Left and Right, is one of the great secondary principles of National Socialism. All occupations and pursuits, all manner of persons and all fields of activity, must be integrated into the corporate life of the community.

The social feeling of oneness must find practical expression in, and in turn be stimulated by, a sincere and profound concern for social and economic justice. Consciousness of kinship and care for the collective good of the folk demand that every citizen must have an equal opportunity to develop and exercise his talents and rise according to his merits; and that every citizen must receive a fair return for his services to the community, and even the simplest worker an assurance of the necessities of life.

Thus, we arrive at the socialist element in National Socialism. This is not the Marxist socialism of state ownership of the means of production and distribution, which is the economic over-government of the ant heap, and as objectionable as the predatory individualism of the capitalist system, which is the economic under-government, or anarchy, of the jungle.

Instead it is Folk Socialism, or the regulation of private enterprise for the equitable division of its fruits, under equitable conditions. The economic injustices and social evils of capitalism have fostered Marxism, with its pernicious form of public control of the economy, and the alternative to both lies in National Socialism.

The folk ideal, which entails the defence of the race, the unity of the nation, and the welfare of the people, engenders National Socialism's principle of leadership and an elite in the service of these objectives.

Its conception of a natural order is one which not only ordains that men are born into the folk for a life within the folk, but also that they possess hereditary differences of capacity to serve the community. Accordingly, for the maximum good of all, the superior must lead the inferior.

The natural leaders must be selected, established as a hierarchic elite under a supreme leader, and empowered to fulfil their function.

Unlike liberalism, National Socialism does not regard the directive power of the state as something essentially repressive, but instead as a great beneficial power of guidance and arbitration, encouragement and protection. It upholds the dictum: "*All for the folk and the folk for all.*" It sanctions whatever means are necessary, in whatever fields, to ensure that everyone and everything in the community is in harmony with this.

It sees the duty of the National Socialist government as the representation of the will of the folk, conceived not as the transitory whim of some democratic mob, but as the higher interest of the community, viewed in historical perspective as a continuity of purpose, embracing not only the general good of the present, but the heritage of the past and the needs of the future as well.

NATIONAL SOCIALISM: WORLD CREED FOR THE FUTURE

With the gigantic catastrophe of 1945, the greatest setback to human evolution in recorded history, still close behind us, its chilling and choking memory still omnipresent, and before us difficulties and disadvantages so gigantic as to deny us any immediate or early prospect of gaining power over our respective countries, what can be done?

One option it may be instantly stated with certainty we do not have in this doleful situation, and whereby it is vastly less doleful than otherwise, is of course to give up.

This is something which a real National Socialist is by nature and by definition utterly incapable of doing because the will to struggle, which is the elixir of National Socialism, is in the very bones of his being.

Without it he would not be who he is, but some spiritual eunuch of the living dead. A real National Socialist is one who, in the last resort, even if it could be proved to him with mathematical certainty that physical defeat would attend all his efforts, would still go on fighting.

He would do so, inflicting as much punishment as possible on the enemy, and with a warrior's song in his heart, because it is his nature to do so, and because a victory of the spirit is always won thereby.

But having ruled out surrender, what else? In the new convulsive decade of the 1980s is National Socialism to become at best the minute defiant echo of a bygone age, a barren exercise in nostalgia, or at worst the puerile mummery of morons and misfits; or is it to be subjected to cosmetic surgery which National Socialism amounts to castration in order to fit the times? Or is there a way in which it can both respond to circumstances with hope of success, and yet retain its integrity?

Now, on the threshold of a new decade, is high time for some careful and comprehensive stocktaking which must begin with a sharp scrutiny and a complete survey of our ideology.

CHANGING AND UNCHANGING CREED

A creed is not, while it thrives, a static conception, but something lifelike, growing in the minds of its upholders. Absolute fixity comes only with what amounts to death and mummification.

The measure of its historical stature, its relevance and consequent longevity, lies in its fusion of the timeless and the time- full, or the extent to which it combines a permanent constancy of basic principle with a supple adaptability of form and method to time and place, along with a capacity to grow by the development of its potentialities. Where adaptability encroaches on basic principle itself, modifying this in the pursuit of expediency, the trespass creates its own penalty in the fatal illusion of quicker and easier success, for the creed itself fails and disappears through dismemberment. Therein lies the blindness and folly of compromise.

On the other hand, where inviolability, which belongs to basic principle, is attached to form and method, and where even that change which is pure progression or germination is denied, then the result is no less disastrous. The creed atrophies and becomes a sterile husk because of this particular confusion of the time-full and the timeless. Therein lies the blindness and folly of rigidity.

There is the further complication that ways and means, however optional and variable otherwise, must be consistent with basic principles and thus ultimate objectives. That the ends justify the means is a facile assertion much misunderstood and misapplied in the absence of its corollary, which is that those means must, ipso facto, be in harmony with those ends, which can logically be nothing other than the fulfilment of the basic principles, in order to receive their justification thereby. In fact, the ends prescribe the means, and the means, determine the actual results. That is the precise interaction. To repeat an old but worthy analogy: you cannot combat cannibalism by consuming cannibals.

ILLUSION IN COMPROMISE

One cannot promote National Socialism by departing from it, either in the sense of discarding or postponing vital aspects of it, as distinct from truly transitory details of time and place, or resorting to methods which are at variance with basic principles. Those who attempt to do so on the pretext of increasing popularity and quickening victory, and with the assurance that there after the real thing will follow, fail to comprehend two facts.

Firstly, they fail to perceive the addictive consequences of compromise, according to which power gained by means of compromise is so likely to be used to retain power by means of compromise.

Secondly, they fail to perceive that the ultimate end or true purpose of National Socialism is not merely a revolution in the state, but a revolution in the minds of men and women. This must begin before and continue after the attainment of authority in the state, and will necessarily be thwarted by any disabling compromise in the course of attaining that authority. In short, power must be gained through National Socialism in order to be sure of the power to implement National Socialism. Otherwise, the great and bitter irony of the exercise is that the nearer and quicker compromise gets you to power, the further it takes you away from your original ideal and objective. So, compromise is indeed a fool's accelerator.

National Socialism today, entering the new decade, is endangered fully as much by those within its nominal ranks who incline to try and modify its essential nature by a compromise of principle or the adopting of a conflicting practice, or to confine it to its antecedents, petrifying it in the time-capsule of the 1930s and the place-capsule of Germany. The Jew at the microphone or the communist at the Street corner is an enemy readily detected and confronted, but the nominal National Socialist with the weakening words of expediency or the fossilised antiquarian outlook is another more insidious and more injurious menace, effectively an enemy within, albeit unconsciously and unintentionally so.

RIGHTISTS AND POPULISTS

There are, those, on the one hand, who seek to reduce National Socialism to something of the so-called "right," stifling its supra-national and pan-Aryan implications to present it as nothing more than a militant form of the old nationalism; suppressing its radical economic and social implications to make it an accomplice of capitalism; thus, depriving it of its revolutionary content in order to accommodate it within the old order which it exists to overthrow and replace.

Alongside them are some who want instead to pervert it into something of the "left" of the old order by distorting its concern for thorough social justice and economic equity to deny that beneficial extent of private enterprise, that justifiable amount of private property, and that essential degree of personal responsibility for one's own welfare which is equally its concern; thus, reducing it to a form of national bolshevism.

In the same business of seeking in one way or another to make our creed acceptable to the old order, and thus to render the remedy harmless to the disease, are those slick practitioners of political perversion who seek to make political "*pop*" out of National Socialism, thus defiling it to death on the plea that they are giving it new life.

In the wanton spirit of feeble confession to feckless fashion, they express the foul and ridiculous heresy that to make progress we have to become like the enemy and copy his abominable ways.

They then proceed to pride themselves in their meretricious cleverness in seeking to' "*modernise*" National Socialism by presenting it as "*with it*," meaning in accordance with the very trends of decadence it exists to eradicate. They even go to the extent of wanting to dress it up literally in the slovenly jeans which are today's uniform of democratic degeneracy, to crown it even with the long scruffy hair of the dissipated rabble of ragamuffins comprising the "*modern*" generation, and to give it as accompaniment even the infernal noise known as "*pop*" which is the authentic flatulence of multiracialism.

This they favour in blind disregard of the fact that smartness of personal appearance is the inevitable expression of that perception of order against chaos as the secret of the universe which is the pith and kernel of our creed, and that the variations of jungle music are abandonment to chaos in sound as contrary to our creed as anything else.

The habits and paraphernalia of abandonment and reversion to the jungle are being deliberately promoted, no less than all the miasmic claptrap of "*permissiveness*" and "*brotherhood*" which goes with them, because of the coarsening and cheapening, spiritually sterilizing and racially dissolvent effect.

Those ultimately responsible for this conditioning of the masses are those for whom there is most profit in an indiscriminate society of banal barbarity, a mongrel herd kept occupied with trivialities and oblivious to ugliness, inspired by the market-cry of the television commercial in its pursuit of electronic happiness as its ethos.

These Elysian fields of bovine contentment constitute the ultimate containment for the goyim in the oncoming Hebrew millennium.

For National Socialism, in mortal conflict with this world wilderness of the zombies, all higher and thus truly human as distinct from animal happiness is not to be sought in itself, but is the satisfaction of fulfilment which is the by-product of service of something greater than self, and wherein courage is the motif, not the superficial and perverse "*kindness*" which is the ubiquitous poisoned sugar in the deadly diet of democracy.

DEALERS IN FLOTSAM AND JETSAM

Parallel with the debasing modernists of National Socialism are the equally debasing patrons of the chronic misfits. Because judicious violence in the true service of National Socialism is justifiable as at one with all the other forms of Nature, and because we National Socialists are rebels against the present society of multiracial democracy, they misinterpret this to sanction association with all sorts of other rebels against this and any and every other society, who, with corresponding misunderstanding, conceive National Socialism to be a haven and stamping ground for their kind.

These dealers in flotsam and jetsam are the sort of people who in Britain today resort to increasing manpower by recruiting the mindless oafs called "skinheads," these tonsured, nihilistic hooligans being against all order, old or new, and for violence for violence's sake and the pure pleasure of damage and destruction.

The argument of the patrons of the vandals and hooligans is, at its least, the simple admission that they think they can make use of the vandalism and hooliganism, which is the old error of the means defeating the ends, for in truth it is the anti-social ones who make use of them.

At its most, it is the claim that the antisocial ones are the helpless victims of environment, and will be drawn to higher purposes by association with them. Now, if the latter was not merely wishful thinking but an actual fact, the experiment could be justified, but then in proportion to its success such as "skinheads" would manifestly cease to be "skinheads," whereas in the instances contemplated they remain basically the same.

The problem is always to convert to us, and not in the process of gaining attention and influence to fall into what amounts to conversion to others.

In the cases in question the acceptance of such elements, while they clearly remain such elements, as members and conspicuous participants in marches and other public events indicates the degree of conversion the wrong way, comparable to the psychiatrist who begins to contract the psychosis of his patient.

The "skinheads" have stayed "skinheads" while the supposed National Socialists have become that much less of authentic National Socialists. It is not the former who have been uplifted, but the latter who have been downgraded by the experiment.

These particular protagonists of popularisation, meaning perversion, have committed the cardinal error of thinking that putting National Socialism on the streets means allowing it into the gutter with the garbage. They have depleted it to a crude and negative racial hatred and for superficial anti-Red confrontation in the mode and mood of a mob of football fans for whom National Socialism is an excuse for a "*punch up*," and the Swastika a gimmick for shock and scare, and a talisman for mayhem.

HOLLYWOOD NAZIS

A different but no less dangerous debasement from within, being an extreme form of that rigidity which fossilises our creed by failing to cultivate freely and fully the implications of its true principles while slavishly conforming to details which can and should be alterable, comes from those politically superficial and primarily theatrical and positively juvenile exponents, who may be termed "Hollywood Nazis."

For these exhibitionists dressing up in the costume of the past, treated as a fetish, and posturing and parading as part of the masquerade provides the pleasure of pretence, which is all it is, although the performance undoubtedly has the psychotherapeutic effect of serving to ease the feeling of inadequacy in its performers, in a manner akin to the African savage who dons the skin of a lion as a mantle in the sure belief that he will thereby become invested with the strength and courage of the king of the jungle.

Akin to these performing political playboys, the fancy dress and regalia freaks with their burlesque show, are those who, in their similar bondage to the outward forms of the past, entomb National Socialism in museum of their minds.

Content to confine it to the collection of relics and records, and to participate simply by association with souvenirs, they treat it as a finished phenomenon only to be contemplated in recollection, whereas National Socialist Germany was not the entire and final happening, but the majestic opening act of a continuous work.

LAW OF NATURE

The National Socialism of the Germany of Adolf Hitler, as expressed by its prime exponents, was the first systematic articulation of the orientation of society in conscious harmony with the discerned laws of Nature, as opposed to the harmful contrary artificialities of all other schools of thought.

Perceiving the constant struggle of Nature which is the assertion of existence itself, and the process of the selection of the fit and the rejection of the unfit which is improvement, it saw in the order and pattern and ultimate harmony of the Universe the essence of beauty, and sought actively to conform to and promote this in the arrangements of Man.

Since Nature is totality, National Socialism could only respond by being a totality of outlook, an attitude to everything, not something limited to the territory of politics, and thus a fragment of life. It could not be less than a cosmic philosophy extending to all parts of life in a coherent structure, the spiritual and the cultural no less than the economic and political, and in consequence generating its own scale of values and distinctive code of ethics.

Thus, distinguishing itself by casting Man as the fulfilling agent instead of the foe of Nature in an entelechy sought and expressed by living life to the full, National Socialism accordingly dedicated itself to the primary role of race in human affairs, parallel to the role of comparable differentiations in all other living things.

It recognised in the human differentiations both between and within the races the working of the great test of Nature which is life itself, and through which suitability and superiority are established, and thus the ascent of Man on the ladder of creation takes place.

In doing so, it observed the paramount civilising potential of the Aryan, the obstructive and destructive capacity of the Jew, the decline which is the result of the mixture of the races, and the great need for and benefit of eugenical action within the race.

Applying this same insight, appreciative of the stimulus and the benefit of competition, to the economic sphere, it upheld private enterprise and private property, personal responsibility which is inseparable from competition, and is the acknowledgement of true freedom and the beginning of leadership in self-leadership, and leadership itself as the duty and privilege of superiority. At the same time the same racial awareness which prompted all this prompted also, and no less a concern from kinship which enjoined the reconciliation of competition with cooperation and social justice. This called for measures to allow a fair start and free play to human worth, to sustain competition by the prevention of abuses including its suppression by monopoly, to ensure a fair reward to all by the prevention of excessive gain to any, to ensure an adequate living in retirement after a useful working life, to confine money to the service of production and consumption, to encourage the health and strength of the people and their native culture, and to preserve all the natural resources and amenities of this world.

This may be said to be the bedrock of belief, the basis of principle of the creed of National Socialism. Anything less than or different from this makes something other than National Socialism.

MASS SUPPORT NOT NOW

With elements so radical and contents so comprehensive, National Socialism was necessarily a revolutionary creed to overthrow and replace the old unnatural order, not to try and reform it to prolong it. Yet, after an unsuccessful coup in its early days, it finally attained power by way of negotiation, not seizure.

While this was in some respects a safer and easier procedure, since the end beyond this means was the achievement of a revolutionary change in society, the inevitable accommodation thereby and thereafter of elements of the old order carried with its grave impediment at the best and downright sabotage at the worst; and thus, made it in other respects a more dangerous and harder procedure.

It may well be a fact that without this accommodation National Socialism would not have come to power at that time, but, if so, it can no less be a fact that because of the consequent hindrance or restraint, the true National Socialist revolution had only just begun, however glorious that beginning, when its opponents from the outside, aided by those on the inside, destroyed it. Furthermore, in the inchoate National Socialist state, far too many nominal National Socialists had only a superficial understanding of the common and simple version of their creed, and no real appreciation of its deeper and ultimate implications. While the terrible shortage of time afforded by destiny makes a powerful excuse for this dilution of the revolution, must we not also consider the mixture of both the masses and the elite in one and the same body, the party, as an error of the past to be avoided in the future?

Our position today is vastly different. We do not possess the support or any near likelihood of the support to make us the necessary bargaining factor to tempt us to any accommodation with the Establishment of the old order, whereby we can be helped to power at the price of impediment to the revolution. Indeed, all the signs are that, unless and until there is a complete breakdown of the old system to administer sufficient of a jolt to the masses to bring them to see sense, they will not come to support National Socialism in sufficient numbers to enable the acquisition of power by any means: election, negotiation, or seizure (which last is in any event only feasible in a breakdown, and then finally justified).

Accordingly, any and all efforts in the present period to muster the masses to provide the necessary support for the attainment of power, including the contesting of elections, are doomed to failure, and are a waste of time, money, and energy; and this, whatever the enfeebling compromises to try and coax them by debasing our creed to fit their present debasement, because we cannot in this outbid the old politicians already in power, even by descending to their level.

Conversely, when the time is ripe this ipso facto, will mean that such will be the mood of the masses that they will not be looking for the compromises of 'moderation," but the "extremism" of emergency measures in an emergency. Only when they are intolerably fed up will they turn against the old order, and only then will they respond to its replacement: National Socialism.

WHAT CHANCE HAVE WE?

Have we, therefore, any real chance of ultimate success? Even with the shrewdest preparation and procedure on our part to take advantage of any and all opportunity, will not the enemy, having learnt the lesson of the 1930s, be competent enough to prevent a sufficient breakdown, including an economic collapse, to give us our breakthrough?

The answer is surely that the chance will be there, inevitably so, because the enemy is committed to the forces of breakdown, with consequent danger that they will be turned against him, in necessarily seeking to tear down old traditions and old standards in the course of creating the ultra-materialistic multiracial mankind which is the common aim of all the parties opposed to National Socialism; and because his economic system has such a high inherent proclivity to crises, however great the desire to keep the cattle contented with sufficient fodder and synthetic fun.

But will the masses move against their master even in extremity, or will their spirit be sapped to submission more than sparked to revolt by the process of misrule. The chance that they will move is heavily related to the fact that, behind its array of illusory liberties, the politics of the enemy in its distinctions of left and right are pre-eminently the politics of the belly. In consequence, if the belly in the comprehensive meaning of material pleasures anticipates or suffers deprivation, then democracy's claim to support evaporates.

What we now have to concentrate on is what lies within our power now as the starting point in the chance of chances, and that is to maximise our own potentialities in accord with prevailing circumstances.

TODAY'S SIX TASKS

.... What does this entail? It entails the following six requirements, and, far from being a matter of gloom, contemporary circumstances should be seen as providing considerable compensation in the ultimate advantage of activities their constraint encourages in response to the exciting challenge of our great adversity.

The lack of short cuts, so prone to be illusory, should oblige our slower advance to be that much more thorough.

Firstly, we have to purify and develop our creed, free from all compromises and omissions of expediency, all confusions, and all contradictions. This is the starting point and matrix of the revolution of the future, and we shall return to this crucial subject in detail shortly.

Secondly, instead of seeking prematurely to mobilise the masses, we have to apply ourselves without this distraction to the prerequisite task which is to build a real elite imbued, as its standard bearers, with our purified and developed creed, and trained as functionaries of the National Socialist state in microcosm in its propagation and implementation. Thereby, in the time of future opportunity, the essential cadres will exist to step forward, trained and dependable, to take charge of events. Thereafter, in the marshalling of the masses both for the attainment of power and for its subsequent utilisation, those masses will not swamp us, and draw us their way, but instead will be harnessed and led our way by our elite. The very futility of seeking to organise the masses in present circumstances and the necessity instead to concentrate on the elite, should really be welcomed, not deplored, as a salutary discipline resulting not only in the development of that vital distillation of leadership, the elite, which hitherto has been impeded, if not frustrated, by the organisation of a party campaigning for mass support; but the formulation for the future of a clear and exclusive division, whatever the nomenclature, between that organisation which embodies the elite, and any organisation which formally enrolls the masses who are by nature only meant to be auxiliaries.

The folly of striving vainly against nature to make regular activists, a natural minority, out of the vast majority of people, and thereby creating a weakness by and from numbers in the illusion that quantity in itself means strength, is a vital lesson to be learned now. Given a real elite, the extent to which lack of numbers can be amply made up for by intensity of belief harder work, greater courage, the acquisition of higher skill, and the employment of greater enterprise, is amazing. Far from a radical, uncompromising creed being injudicious in the present period, it will desirably frighten away the unsuitable many, and attract the desirable minority.

Thirdly, the acquisition of total national power, at one go, being at present out of reach, we must meanwhile give our attention to the acquisition of power in other lesser and more gradual ways. We must take note of, and practice as far as possible, the art of making revolution by infiltration, gaining power piecemeal by stealth, being successfully practiced by our opponents. Those who say that communism cannot come in this or that country because of its inability to do so by the overt means of the ballot box or a march on the capital are blind to the fact that power can also be gained bit by bit, slowly but no less surely, through the infiltration of persons to positions of power in all fields and at all levels, and the exercise then of the influence these positions provide. It is happening right now in country after country where a creed of multiracial equality and collectivism, which amounts to a very substantial first instalment of communism, accompanied by encouragement to many aspects of barbarity as a corrosive to facilitate the revolution in view, is being purveyed by the deliberate agents of infiltration. With Britain today, communism is not something outside her gates, or restricted within to its overt adherents, but is already functioning in the press, radio, and television, in the race relations and social security networks, and in the schools and the trade unions, because of the number of Reds who have taken power there. Obviously, we are severely handicapped in comparison, but not to the exclusion of all possibilities.

Fourthly, as another form of power snatching in bits and pieces, even if very small bits and pieces, we must give due attention to the promotion of all possible piecemeal implementations now of National Socialism in microcosm as an infiltration of our society of the future into the society of today. For instance, where National Socialists can set up schools for the education of their children, even as additions where they cannot be substitutes for the orthodox ones; labour service projects for their teenage sons and daughters; business enterprises on thorough National Socialist lines; even whole miniature local communities: in all such we can today anticipate and experiment with our system of the future. Some such projects can have application and benefit to the local area and the local people in general, and, since practice is more potent propaganda than preaching, can lay foundations for future support; while at the same time benefitting us by providing experiment for prototypes in preparation for the future. In this present period, when desires and efforts to grasp at the state as a whole and at the top are unrealistic, the new radical National Socialism has to show itself by its appropriate concentration on the roots of society, capturing ground from the democratic state at the bottom as it can. The full extent to which society can be changed short of national state power is a matter which must be thoroughly investigated and appreciated, and then exploited to the utmost.

Fifthly, attention must be given to those deeds of high imagination, high daring, high organisation, which have a proportionately high propaganda impact, winning attention beyond mere words which come cheaply, sensationally asserting the existence of the Movement now and staking its claim for the future in a period when ordinary campaigning for the attention and support of the masses is unprofitable and hence to be eschewed. These are activities which call for the elite and in turn attract people suitable for the elite, and keep the sword bright and sharp, so that there is no question of a withdrawal from mass activity being a retreat to a political hermitage, which is indeed a very real danger to be guarded against. At their, highest development it may be said to be a matter of applying the principles of Otto Skorzeny to political warfare, whereby small elite groups of specially trained men can through the use of the most unconventional audacity achieve results vastly in excess of their numbers. Our creed is the creed which upholds quality above quantity in life, and, especially in these days when quantity is so obviously not on our side or near at hand, it behoves us to concentrate on the powerful art of making quality make up for that lack of numbers.

Finally, since we need the breakdown of the old order to build the new, the more spanners which can be thrown in the works of the present system, the better. Its systematic sabotage in every possible way is purposeful commendable demolition for the real National Socialist revolutionary, who appreciates that things have got to get worse before they get better, and that an existing decrepit structure has to be torn down before a new and better edifice can be erected in it's a place.

At first glance, however, this might be taken to pose a dilemma by carrying the suggestion that decadence itself is to be encouraged and promoted, but it is resolved by adherence to the criterion that National Socialism as the end justifies all means consistent with National Socialism, but none other.

DEVELOPMENT OF DOCTRINE

To return, now, to the first and foremost of our six great tasks for the 1980s in detail, this may be defined as the pursuit of that revolution of the mind which is the precursor of that revolution in the state leading to the revolution in society. It involves exploring, examining, distinguishing, and declaring the entirety of our creed 'in its fullest and deepest implications, devoid of the dilutions of expediency, as a pure product of the reason and the spirit.

It then extends to its application in the formulation of schemes and measures to meet the forthcoming problems of our countries and their communities, so that the eternal voice of National Socialism sounds not aged from afar, but youthful from at hand. In this projection of principles, which are outside and above time and place, to compatible applications in time and place we have to show that National Socialism, not being in principle something peculiar to Germany and the 1930s, but instead universal and ageless, is therefore as native to America and Britain as anywhere else, and as timely relevant now as in the past. In all of this there is much to be done. In doing this we have to investigate and decide the presentation of our creed in the most persuasive form consistent with all its essentials.

This, it needs emphasising, is the subtle art of bringing people to accept those essentials, and nothing other or less than them, in contrast to compromise which is the omission of essentials in order to secure support, and thereby for something different. In one and the same process, based on the same penetrating analysis of the mind of the outsider, we have to formulate and perfect our counter-arguments to the hostile arguments of our opponents. In this we have to succeed in showing that National Socialism, far from being the denial of freedom and justice as depicted by its opponents and believed by the masses, is in truth the optimum increase of both. Hitherto, the power of our opponents and the apathy of the masses have been made the excuse far too much for the downright incompetence of post-war National Socialist presentation which has been woefully unimaginative and clumsy. In this and our propaganda as a whole, which can be decisive in the battle for the mind, our aim must be to learn to be professionally proficient, and even better than our successful opponents.

SPIRITUAL SIGNIFICANCE

In our doctrinal introspection, the life-embracing extent of National Socialism as the creed of man's conformity to Nature necessarily gives rise to the conception of Man as a functioning aspect of the cosmos, in its great eternal rotational process of growth and decay. In this being, which is both changeful and continuative, death is no absolute extinction, but a transformation whereby the decomposition of one life-form results in the composition of some new life-form, and thus the beginning of a new cycle.

From the soil and its atmosphere, we spring by way of its elements and products, on which, directly or indirectly, we depend and which become part of us, and to the soil and its atmosphere we return. To ascribe this earthbound state to Man is not to belittle him, as the believers in a soul which lives on and migrates to a heaven in the sky after the death of the body will contend. Instead it is to evaluate him no less highly in revering Nature that much more by appreciation of his total involvement, which is infinite and eternal, in Nature.

It is not to reduce him to some crude hedonistic materialism, but, in rejection of this, to exalt him in an idealism of this world which is spiritual. Our cosmic conception of Man, and the struggle which is the meaning of life in its urge for achievement as the expression of identity, the courage against adversity which achievement demands and which is will, the voice of identity, the satisfaction in achievement which is the higher form of happiness, and the role of Race in its fullest sense in this struggle of life: this inevitably constitutes a compulsive scale of values and a consequent code of ethics.

What fulfils Nature; what benefits the race as the servant of Nature; what benefits National Socialism as the servant of the race; are good: what does not is bad. That which truly seeks and secures this good is right. That which does not is wrong.

No other command contrary to this can be accepted by National Socialists. Otherwise there is no National Socialism. Now all this of course rightly raises National Socialism to a religious level, and a question which National Socialists have got to face up to and resolve in the 1980s, as part of their promotion of the revolution of the mind, is whether this is really compatible with what is really Christianity, and, if not, whether now is the time to say so.

CHRISTIANITY'S INCOMPATIBILITY

It will immediately be objected by some, if not many, that to open up this issue is divisive, and, moreover, at a time of acute numerical weakness when we desperately need all, the adherents and friends we can obtain.

But surely it does not in the long run make for greater strength to maintain an ideological weakness, attempting to reconcile the irreconcilable, even if tacitly so; and surely now is the time to build strongly for the future with clear, courageous, and consistent thought, discarding the contradictions and the inhibitions and the cobwebs.

Certainly, there are many otherwise good, and even very good, men and women who somehow, in a blind spot in their minds, manage to allow National Socialism and Christianity to cohabit.

One would hate to hurt them, let alone alienate any of them. Yet, if, as must be, the logic of our creed, and thereby its integrity of character, is our paramount consideration, then surely, we must, seek in every patient and pleasant way to bring them to see that Christianity is inevitably opposed to National Socialism, whatever some of its nominal followers may think and do to the contrary.

Christianity is committed to multiracialism because its Jesus Christ, who is its entire justification, sanctioned and promoted racial equality and racial brotherhood, which in turn sanction and promote racial integration and racial interbreeding, when he proclaimed that all mankind, regardless of race, is equal in the eyes of its god.

Thereby it is devoted to an anti-Aryan purpose, whatever the contortions of those who try to give it an Aryan look, and whereby people are diverted into a crippling morass of biblical reference and interpretative conjecture.

In addition, its guilt complex of original sin; its servile message of docility; its belief in a deity who is omnipotent and omniscient and who nevertheless tolerates the most obvious and indisputable and grossest injustices; and its anti-eugenic conception of sanctity and compassion for all human life as God-given: all this, which is an integral part of Christianity, is demonstrably at variance with the thought and spirit of National Socialism.

Accordingly, Christianity cannot be the religion for us, and needs to be rejected now as such.

Otherwise, it is bound sooner or later to cause disruptive problems of allegiance, and inspire debilitating inhibitions, which will most gravely handicap us in our struggle for power, and will create trouble galore for us on coming to power, as happened before in Germany.

There Hitler bought needed support it is true in return for restraint on this fundamental issue, but had to pay a terrible price for it in the long run.

To reject Christianity without putting anything in its place would be to exchange one error for another, and so would any attempt to replace it with the dead form of some ancient paganism which would be an artificial and barren imposition.

While we can and should indeed relate our religious outlook to our pre-Christian heritage with its substantial similarity, this outlook is a precise paganism which belongs to National Socialism, being entirely generated by National Socialism. It has to be expressed in contemporary forms and terms as a reflection of the present world order to be relevant and so to thrive.

BATTLE OF THE ARTS

Along with recognising and pursuing its implications even to the extent of religion, we have to present and emphasize all the cultural implications of this life-wide creed of ours.

The total war is to be fought on all fronts, and to the neglect of none. All art forms can either be in accord with National Socialism as expressive of harmony and order, or in conflict with it in departure from these qualities.

Just as the sublime grandeur of the music of Wagner is pure National Socialism in sound, so is the primitively repetitive and diabolically discordant din of "pop," particularly in its extreme forms, anti-NS chaos in this medium; and its hideous purveyors are to attacked as fiercely as any renegade politician or race mixing cleric in theirs.

Likewise, the mess-daubing of "modern" painting is chaos in line and colour, and thus an expression of anti-National Socialism.

Likewise, the indeterminate shapes of "modem" sculpture are anti-National Socialism in whatever the material used. Their deranged perpetrators are part of the multifarious array of the active enemy. Those persons who call themselves National Socialists, but at least tolerate these forms of decadence in their perniciously partial and superficial understanding and acceptance of our creed, if they do not actually dabble in them themselves, are not really on our side, and we would be better off without them as they are.

REPRESENTATION AND CRITICISM

In advocating leadership with its personal responsibility instead of the collective irresponsibility and inertia which characterises and condemns democracy, providing the opportunity for great vested interests and alien elements to rule by manipulation from behind the scenes, it is not enough to cite the superlative qualities and achievements of Adolf Hitler.

Of him there has been one, and one no more. It is incumbent on us to devise a system of honest and effective representation of the people, consistent with true leadership, whereby it is clear that we uphold this form of freedom for the people, and that we reject democracy precisely because it fails to provide this while pretending to do so.

In the course of this, proper provision must be made for the succession in the event of death, incapacity, or downright failure of the Leader, in the understanding that this planet can hardly hope to be lucky enough to be presented with a second Hitler in the immediate future.

Another problem that National Socialism in this preparatory period of searching review has to resolve is the adjudication of the National Socialist State as the zealous promoter of the National Socialist good between the advantages and disadvantages of so-called "free speech."

To allow the propagation of what is distinctly and seriously harmful, according to the National Socialist view, is clearly abhorrent and impossible, but seriously harmful too can be any suppression of justifiable criticism, and the protection this undoubtedly gives to abuses and defects. We have to determine and justify the precise position we propose to adopt in this respect, bearing in mind that bans and punishments should be the last resort, and the fewer the better, being an admission of the failure of National Socialism in obtaining the end by other and earlier means; and that any appearance of being unable to face the arguments of opponents in open controversy is undesirable.

ECONOMIC HARMONY

Another important field for the formulation of extended National Socialism to fit our own times and places is that of industrial relations.

Here we have to be able to detail a permanent remedy for the continual conflict and perpetual strikes ravaging the economy in Britain and other countries, and of a nature which disposes of the Marxist argument that National Socialism is the servant or ally of capitalism.

All workers' and employers need to be bound by some contract of employment under some charter of industry which accords to each both the rights and the obligations of their positions, including that of arbitration, which excludes strikes and lock-outs as outdated demonstrations of economic anarchy; which provides for workers' representation throughout the community; and for workers shares in the profits of the firm.

Along with this introduction of just and mutually beneficial economic government in the place of internecine chaos, there needs to be the abolition of those schemes of the misnamed "Welfare State" which, whatever they may provide from the public purse by way of general taxation, take away personal responsibility, breed dependence, and encourage the lazy and improvident to exploit the industrious and thrifty.

Instead, the system of the National Socialist State should ensure, after exaction of proportionately less taxation, an adequate net wage to everyone who does an adequate day's work, and then require its citizens to assume responsibility for themselves, and pay their way; and, in respect of any special assistance needed in an emergency, ultimately to repay its provision. The double-headed dictum of National Socialist economic justice should thus be: no one shall want through no fault of his own, and no one shall gain through no effort of his own. This does not of course preclude any and all social provisions based on a direct and adequate personal contribution.

In all its economic and social plans, the true development of National Socialism is, and has to be shown and stressed as, something neither of capitalism nor Marxism, being not for one class or the other, or any section whatsoever, but for the whole community; and based not on a cash nexus but on the bond of race. Because of this, we National Socialists in fulfilling and asserting this revolutionary distinction have relentlessly to reject being labelled as some kind of right-wing nationalists. Being no part of the old order, we are against it right, left, and centre.

National Socialism: Vanguard of the Future

NATIONAL SOCIALISM NOT NATIONALISM

We have not only to avoid deviation into confusion with right wing nationalism in its economic and social aspects. We have also, to break free from, reject, and rise above that right-wing nationalism in its external aspect which up to now has been so much confused with and so greatly compromised and corrupted National Socialism, deforming it to tremendous loss.

We have to go forward into the future with a dynamic answer both to the nationalism and the internationalism of both capitalism and Marxism. That answer must be the world-wide call of Aryan kinship to create, above all lesser attachments and divisions of class and country, a real community of united Aryan peoples. Nothing less than this is the maturity of our creed in the fulfilment of its implications of the Aryan "folk."

It may be that National Socialism had in the 1930s to find its beginning and make its early way through a resurgence of nationalism as the route of the times, and indeed to take this into its very title for its folkism as a matter of contemporary convenience rather than eternal aptness of definition. Yet, from our vantage point today, it cannot be denied that, if nationalism was utilised to carry it forward, the same nationalism reacted to hold it back. We serve our creed best today not by pretending that everything was perfect in the past, which is the way to confine it to the past and deprive it of a future, but by recognising any errors or imperfections from a National Socialist point view, providing this is done with ample reason and in perspective within a context of overall appreciation of the nevertheless gigantic achievements of the past, and constructively in order thereupon to correct and improve.

"*National Socialism is not for export*," as a pronouncement attributed to the Third Reich, may well have served certain purposes, including the major truth that each particular country needed to evolve its own particular form.

But taken, as it may so very easily be done, as the confinement of the whole doctrine to one people, one country, and one time, this total endorsement of exclusive local nationalism is an appalling deformation of true National Socialism.

JEWISH WEAPON OF WAR

This restrictive element of the old nationalism, which probably prevailed most of the time among the adherents of the German National Socialism of the 1930s, did immense harm to its prospects in reducing the power of its appeal to those outside

National Socialism: Vanguard of the Future

Germany to join in preventing the move to war, and, after the war had broken out, to side with Germany in a European New Order.

At the same time, it was reflected in the forms of professed National Socialism which arose in other countries. In Britain, the same old nationalism led Mosley, after so commendably opposing the move to war, to exhort his followers, after it had broken out and the testing time had come, not to hinder the conduct of the war against Germany.

It led to most of his followers, in fact, actively aiding the war against National Socialism, many of them in the Forces; and to followers of his even now proudly upholding this in their favour.

That insane fratricidal inter-Aryan war, which brought about the physical downfall of what, despite any and all shortcomings, was most certainly the finest achievement so far of the self-conscious Aryan spirit and will, was the result of German and other European and Aryan nationalism exploited by Jewish international racialism.

This is the monumental lesson to be learned now, at long last, and never henceforth to be forgotten. Never must it happen again! The remedy can be nothing other than the emergence of Aryan international racialism, leading to the unity of the whole Aryan folk.

Though the old, restricted nationalism still pervaded not only the great bulk of the German population under National Socialism, but also the great bulk of party members, and the great bulk of German National Socialist exposition, the new extended racialism of the future, which is the fullest flowering of our creed, and our task now to propagate, showed itself appropriately in that part of the German movement which was its highest elite.

The foremost leaders and thinkers of the ᛋᛋ were distinctly pan-Aryan in their outlook, and this outlook was reflected in the formations of European volunteers which the ᛋᛋ sponsored, and possessed by the best of those volunteers themselves.

Then, theirs was the vision which in time and force could have won the war. Now, theirs is the vision with which in the future the defeat of 1945 can be made but a lost battle in a continuing war which ends in our total and everlasting victory. This will be so, if the National Socialist elite, which is what the National Socialist movement of the present and the future must be, will embrace it wholeheartedly, and carry it forward fanatically.

FOLK COMES FIRST

A racialism which is purblindly partial is not good enough. The racial nationalist who keenly invokes racial factors relating to the nation, and then stops short, and equally keenly turns his back in purblind partiality on the way in which the same racial factors proclaim an entity above and beyond the nation, is a self-destructive and split personality.

The existing nation-states, to whatever extent they are now or have been homogenetic racial units, arose in the course of migrations and divisions of the great race, and are only one form of folk community, and no divinely ordained highest and final form as the myopic nationalists in Britain and elsewhere try to make out.

For us they can only have merit to the extent to which, like everything else, they serve and do not hamper and harm the race, and that the whole race and nothing less than the whole race, the entire Aryan folk.

The Aryan folk preceded all forms of state in the past, and now must take precedence over all existing forms of state in order that it may survive unprecedented perils by proceeding to its coalescence, and thus reunion, in a culminant world community of united states.

Let us not be too small to respond to such a great imperative of history! If we are, we shall instead contribute to that titanic catastrophe whereby, ultimately, the Aryans become extinct like the dinosaurs. This must be the parting of the ways between the mere nationalists and the National Socialists. Now must be an end to any illusion that we are in the same broad camp, and that we are fighting side by side in the same broad cause. The distinguishing gap between us which cannot be bridged is that on the determinant issue of race we belong to and fight for the whole in unity, and not, as they do, for one part against the other parts.

This does not mean for one moment that our concern for that part, our own nation, and that territory, our own country, which are the most native and tangible to us, is lost in a vague concern for others and elsewhere, or truly made lesser or insignificant in consequence.

It means instead that, in realising that they are truly part of something which as a whole is greater we care for them and serve them best in far-sighted relation to that whole, instead of detachment and isolation. Top emphasis now has to be put on the top, which is the whole, for the sake of all the parts, and the parts served through devotion to the whole instead of concentration on the part to the detriment of the whole. In this way, henceforth, nationalism must be seen not as a means of National Socialism, but as the negation of National Socialism.

WHITE PEOPLES OF THE WORLD, UNITE!

We must each and all of us now take the great step forward into the future of firmly and avowedly, without hesitation or reservation, pledging allegiance to the entire Aryan folk as the apex of our creed to which it is inherently dedicated; and this above all other loyalties.

This we must do in explicit and positive rejection of the nationalists, who put country above folk and creed; alongside and equal to our rejection of the Marxists, who put class above race.

We have to accept that in the last resort, if we are obliged to choose between loyalty to folk and creed and loyalty to country contrary to this, we can only choose the first. There our supreme allegiance must lie.

This will make us in the eyes and words of other traitors, traitors to what they stand for, which is not what we stand for, but it will never make us traitors to our rightful allegiance which we freely recognise and accept, and beyond which there is no other due from us.

William Joyce was the executed loyalist to his folk and creed at the price of so-called "treason" to his (nominal) country. He was ever a truer champion of the true interests of the real British people than the unhanged traitor to our race, Winston Churchill.

This bold step of crystal-clear logic will be the sign of the emancipation and emergent maturity of a National Socialism fit to contest and conquer in the future.

Let the cry now go forth loud and clear that we National Socialists are not nationalists, not right-wing patriots, not conservative reformers, but revolutionary racialists summoning the white peoples of the world to unite for survival and supremacy!

Only with a world creed as wide as the whole race, and as wide as the whole of life, can we match our world enemies and thus have the chance to attain full power, and in the world of tomorrow the only full power is world power.

Only National Socialist world supremacy will suffice. Either we and our ideas or our enemies and theirs will dominate the globe.

The revolution of the mind which has to begin before all else, and which is the pure development of our creed to the full, whereby it has the capacity to win the world, is a revolution which begins now in you with your comprehension and acceptance of it.

III. INTO THE FUTURE: THE NATIONAL SOCIALIST VANGUARD

Perhaps the most controversial and yet the most important of Colin Jordan's writings are those which deal with building an effective revolutionary movement which can seize power. These essays and articles are written with the British political scene in mind but they can be applied with little or no modification to the United States or any Aryan land.

"Building the Vanguard" is excerpted from a longer essay of the same name which first appeared in the November, 1981, issue of Colin Jordan's newsletter, "Gothic Ripples". In it, the author discusses the psychological attributes required of a National Socialist revolutionary, and gives practical recommendations on the training of Movement cadres and the building of local cells.

"Party Time Has Ended" is reprinted from the National Review. Here Jordan further develops his conception of the National Socialist Vanguard task force as the necessary alternative to conventional party politics.

"Train of Thought" was privately printed by the author in booklet form in 1989. In it he continues his thoughts on building and training an elite National Socialist vanguard, with special emphasis on recruitment and hypothetical activities. —*Editor*

BUILDING THE VANGUARD

The first requirement of the true elitist is the will power to turn his back on the tempting but futile distractions of ordinary politics, and the second is to purge his mind of all attachment to the existing state and system and society, abstracting himself to the utmost from the grip of this alien world so as to be in total rebellion against its decadence, becoming a fragment of the future.

The latter demands devotion to an advanced degree of self- education in at least all of the basic knowledge of a mentally- equipped elitist, including an insight into the historical context of our struggle; an appreciation of all the major facets of the correlated and universally-prevalent degeneration (the cultural and social and biological and spiritual no less than the plainly political), necessary for that wholeness of view essential for the fullness of combat of the complete belligerent; and an adequate knowledge of relevant law, police procedure, methods of hostile infiltration and provocation and corruption and intimidation, and security precautions against this.

After—and only after—this comes that specialisation in any of the great variety of skills legitimately useful to the true elitist in building the elite now, or acting now against the System to hasten its breakdown, or preparing for action in that eventual situation. In all of this not only has the elitist the task of training to become as far as possible a self-contained unit of the revolution, but, as one becomes joined to others in a gradually evolving corporate structure, that structure has to become more and more the state of the future, developing in advance within the declining body politic of the present. Here we are essentially concerned with the study and application of positive arts and sciences, not in the desultory dabbling of dilettantes, and this involves work galore for those concerned.

Training thus professionally for the struggle, the political soldier of the vanguard needs to articulate a credo whereby each day becomes dedicated to life; on a higher plane. In this, struggle is to be accepted as the assertion of self in the purpose of life, loyalty and courage and strength in struggle as the supreme virtues; the folk—the community of the race—as greater than self, and the highest end; good and evil as precisely what benefits or harms the folk, and nothing else; and race and our beliefs in support of our Race, seen in its entirety, as transcending the geography of countries and the structures of states, there lying our highest allegiance and with, in consequence, every fighter for our Race and our beliefs anywhere in the world being our comrade.

In the beginning you may be alone in all this, an isolated revolutionary agent in enemy-occupied territory. If so, understand at once that this is no cause for lament and despondency, and no excuse for inhibition and inaction, but the very test of initiation as to your suitability because the true elitist is precisely the one capable of operating on his own, if needs be, not the dependent weakling who needs some pre-existing organisation to take him by the hand and arrange things for him. Thus, the initial isolation of a person or a couple of persons is highly salutary, and those who because of this lapse back into the life of the ordinary political herd are exactly those who are incapable and unsuitable for the exacting role of the elite.

Therefore, cast out any feelings of helplessness by uncovering the power which lies within you, the power to make yourself a most effective weapon!

Be confident in the superiority of quality against quantity, whereby the trained and experienced elitist can have an effect far beyond that of the little people on which conventional politics rely! Be assured that numbers are more than anything else an illusion, whenever regardless of quality, being weakness masquerading as strength! Realise that the greatest force in the world is the power of the will residing in the excellence of the few!

Believe this: a tiny minority which is good enough—dedicated enough, knowledgeable enough, trained enough, organised enough—can move mountains, and can topple the vulnerable edifice of the complicated modern state!

But of course, having said that, it has also to be stressed that we need as many as there are of the right people, and so the task of each and every elitist, along with self-development, is to contact and recruit and co-ordinate our kind.

This is essentially a matter of the most careful personal approach, only seeking out those who have already proven themselves suitable, recruiting by invitation, and never in the indiscriminate manner of mass organisations by advertising or canvassing at large. Thus, never seek to bring in somebody who is truly a stranger, recommending himself only by his claims of inclination.

It is here, paradoxically, that existing organisations will be useful to us by bringing people together and exhibiting their worth so that we can conveniently watch and select. In doing so, however, constant vigilance is necessary to avoid for the sake of this access to recruits becoming involved in conventional activities at the cost of our proper pursuits.

In recruitment and operation there can be no room for illogical and wasteful divisions detrimental to an endeavour seeking to draw massive additional strength from that intensity or unity which results from a profound harmony of minds.

Just as there is no place for the barriers of nationality, so, too, is there no room for any exclusion or relegation of women as inferior, this contrary to a recognition of the equal, joint and complementary worth of both sexes, despite some differing capabilities.

Similarly, there is no room for friction between the generations when you are best to be judged as old as you are young in heart, and as young as you are useful; and no place for class cleavage where the only demarcation which really matters is between us and the rest.

In organisation it is imperative to proceed on the basis of small local cells of six or so, this dispersal offering the highest prospect of security, while providing a suitable size of operational unit; and with the maximum autonomy consistent with unified purpose and concerted action.

PARTY TIME HAS ENDED: THE CASE FOR POLITICS BEYOND THE PARTY

We live in the twilight days of a doomed age. Enveloping us is a sick society, condemned to death in the cosmic cycle of transformation by its inherent inability to overcome its strains and stresses: an old order now exhibiting a myriad manifestation of its advancing disintegration.

Yet its final demise may be long delayed, and meanwhile its committed adherents tighten their hold on power, exercised through the veiled force of censorship and indoctrination, and the denial of facilities to opponents, and an increasing resort to coercion and suppression.

These conditions specify a life and death struggle for those dedicated to the survival and advancement of Higher Man through a New Order of Aryandom. In such a struggle the prerequisite for effective action is a searching appraisal of way and means. All practices and procedures must be subjected to an analysis of cost-effectiveness, and retained or rejected accordingly.

Against that back-cloth, this article is concerned to show that the day of the political party is over in its appeal to the masses with leaflets at large, its marches round and round the houses, and all the rest of its routine designed to woo and win the majority vote of the population at an election is hopelessly unproductive.

The political party, whatever its content, and even where nominally anti-democratic, is the organisational product of the mass society called "Democracy," meaning a society which purports to respond to and provide for the Common Man.

It was preceded by the overt and avowed rule of minorities, and Democracy is no less subject to minorities than any other experienced or conjectured society, its only distinction in this respect being that of the modus operandi of its minorities.

It is—except when mortally menaced, and thus brought to a departure from the normal form—mainly manipulative and masked, as opposed to being mainly and blatantly coercive. This dominance of minorities is to be expected as a fact of life. The rule of the public, apart from minute units of administration, has never existed, and never can and never will exist. Civilisation, its management and its finer fruits, has always come not from the Common but from the Uncommon Man.

To say so in no way detracts from the argument for the just apportionment of its material benefits to the former, however lowly in ability and effort and consequent due. By the term "the masses," as used here, is meant not a material but a mental class,

81

regardless of monetary means, made up of the entirety of sheepish citizenry in its conformity to the status quo ordained and blessed by the media of Democracy.

DEMOCRACY'S CONTROL BOX

The political party came into use in the early days of the development of the mass society, consequent on the increase in communication among the people at large, and the increase in the uniformity of their lives, both resulting from the Industrial Revolution, and this long before the advent of the most modern and the most powerful means of moulding the minds of the masses: television.

With television today, the ruling minorities of Democracy have an instrument of mind control in the centre of virtually every home in the land, ensuring that millions upon millions of beguiled boobs of the cathode-ray tube think the "democratic" way, and thus come to vote for the "democratic" options. The total content of the television box today decides the total result of the ballot box tomorrow.

The party game is thus firmly under the power of the enemy of national and racial resurgence, and indulgence in it by those excluded from television, along with the rest of the mass media, is a waste of time.

Even Hitler—who came to power just before his opponents gained this weapon—could not today succeed against and without the magic box. Short of acquiring it for ourselves, or destroying it for the others, there is only one way its all-pervasive, hypnotic, malignant influence can be overcome, and that is through a thorough breakdown in society sufficiently painful to prod the people out of their coma of enslavement.

Created for and concerned with the masses, the nationalist or National Socialist party inevitably becomes crippled and corrupted by the exactions of the involvement. In the delusive pursuit of numbers as the measure of strength, it commits two errors of cardinal severity which guarantee its weakness. Firstly, in its desire to attract the Common Man in quantity, it has to set its requirements of membership at a sufficiently low level, so as to offer him the gratification of identification with a supposedly lofty cause on the basis of little, if anything, more than some paltry payment.

Having brought him into the fold, instead of just taking the collecting box to him on the outside, and with his contribution clearly proving insufficient to enable desirable progress, there follows a constant striving to try and coax him into doing more, which is the folly of trying to make a political activist out of a being whose nature prohibits it.

National Socialism: Vanguard of the Future

Thus, the role of the political party runs counter to that iron law of humanity which decrees that political activists are and always will be a tiny minority, most productive on their own, and that the rest of mankind is and always will be of the nature of political bystanders.

In consequence, while necessarily starting out as a nucleus of political activists, the party soon ends up dissipating the capacity of its activists because of their attachment to the others. Because of this attachment an endless effort ensues to try and keep the recruited men of the masses content with their membership. Activities to this end have to be arranged all over the country, costly in time and money, including all the travelling back and forth by all concerned, primarily to the benefit of the petrol companies, the coach companies, and British Railways.

Beyond this, to a considerable extent the party tends to degenerate into as much as a party of fun and games as anything else, greatly occupied with the posturing and pretending, the babbling and the boozing of the bulk of its members.

PITFALLS OF THE PARTY GAME

The second great error of the party is to set its bounds of beliefs so wide in pursuit of numbers that it achieves thereby not a greater strength but a lesser one through the disunity these spells.

The amalgamation of numbers without a fusion of minds is but a congregation of bodies doomed to discord and disruption, because it is only the semblance and not the substance of unity, which always depends upon a clear predominance of common belief.

With its arms thrown open too widely in welcome, the party, in the width of its policy, takes in differences too large to digest. Along with the positive protagonists of ideological disagreement, it attracts a swamping influx of little people—little in the limitations of their mind, vision, and spirit— saturated with all the superficial perceptions and shallow sentiments of Democracy; people who fancy a spare-time hobby of rebellious radicalism, albeit shackled with the mental fetters of Democracy's notions of "respectability" and "moderation," and thus incapable of dangling more than a couple of toes in the cauldron of revolutionary thought and action.

With the fatal combination of low requirements of membership and wide bounds of policy, the political party can do nothing other than present a feeble spectacle of the tail wagging the dog.

Any complete computation of the cost-effectiveness of this party game, namely what is actually gained from all the relatively inactive but disproportionately vociferous recruits in this forlorn hunt for mass membership, in return for all the constant effort to retain them, condemns the practice completely.

It is said that every little bit helps. So it does, providing and only providing it does not cost as much or more to obtain than it is worth; and providing it is recognised that little bits will never bring victory in a mighty struggle, even when much multiplied. Otherwise, we commit the folly of subscribing to the egalitarian vanity that little is lovely. To do so is to create a slough of frustration wherein the active few are nullified and discouraged by having to carry on their back the burden of the relatively inactive many all around them. The issue here is not for one moment that the little bits of help from the public at large should be scorned and disregarded, but that they can and should be gathered on the outside by the political activists, segregated as a *task force*; and do not need to be and should not therefore be sought through common membership of one and the same organisation as happens with a political party.

BALLOT BOX FUTILITY

The very *raison d'etre* of a political party is to appeal sufficiently to the masses so as to obtain sufficient votes in elections as to attain state power, and thus to form a government of the country.

Nationalist parties have been operating for decades to this end, and have yet failed to obtain or even come near to obtaining a single seat in Parliament, let alone a necessary majority in Parliament, meaning hundreds of seats. While during those decades the plight of our race and nation has worsened and worsened, such parties have come no nearer success.

Some seek to account for this obvious failure to become sufficiently known and acceptable to the masses as a failure to trim policy sufficiently for this political market, including a failure to avoid the stigma of "Nazi" and "extremist."

Their remedy is to convert themselves that much more to the masses, instead of seeking to convert the masses to them, thus seeking to compete with the established parties on their own ground by coming closer to them, while still lacking all the advantages of infrastructure which those orthodox parties possess. Such people, priding themselves on their astuteness, perpetrate the absurdity of abandoning the capacity to reform in pursuit of the opportunity to reform.

In deep privacy and with a crafty wink, some will confide that their contortions are only window-dressing, and that when in power they will show their true colours. Their true colours, apparent enough already, amount to constitutional weakness.

Such are the workings of such frailty that, giving way to it now, come the pay-off they would never have the strength to transcend it. The smears they fear and vainly attempt to distance themselves from are but the concomitant of all adequate proposals for national and racial resurgence, avoidable only by a shameful procedure of self-sterilization.

Others of sterner stuff concede that electoral success is out of reach, but argue that electioneering is nevertheless justified for the sake of the resulting publicity and recruitment.

However, to prove their point they need to show, and fail to show, that the gain in whatever quantity and quality of support resulting from such electioneering at least equals, if not exceeds, the gain to be achieved through an equal expenditure of time and money in other ways.

One thing that electioneering certainly does not achieve is that manifestation which more than that of intellect and ideals moves the masses—the manifestation of strength—for it almost always results in a miserable manifestation of weakness.

Our mis-rulers, secure in their mastery of the media and thereby the minds of the electorate, are comparatively content— if they cannot dispel or deter all resistance— to let Democracy's dissidents expend themselves in the attrition of the party game they have devised and dominate. They are confident that, if by some fluke, these non-conformists did happen to become a real threat, they could increase the array of existing impediments to the extent of a ban in all but name.

Democracy's deceit is all the time to proclaim to its spellbound public the prevalence of freedom, while preventing its exercise by a combination of contrivances.

In this conspiracy of suppression, the current revision of the Public Order Act is intended to turn the screw that much tighter on any Nationalist or National Socialist party as to almost paralyses it.

Even if a veritable miracle happened, and such a party did gain a majority of votes, can you believe that Democracy's masters, faced with elimination, would accept the verdict of the ballot box, and meekly hand over control? A naked struggle would still ensue. It is not some option for us, but an ultimate necessity in any eventuality.

ROLE OF THE TASK FORCE

The corollary of all this is the conclusion that, in so far as the support of the masses is needed in one form or another for the attainment of state power in one way or the another, this can only be obtained through a breakdown of the society of the old order so substantial as to galvanise the docile slaves of the silver screen into a rejection of their enslavers.

Thus today, in place of political parties fantasising about the mobilisation of the mesmerised masses, we need to adopt and develop the conception of the task force or elite organisation of activists engaging only in cost-effective activities to undermine the fraudulent and disastrous system of Democracy in the conviction that through the high quality of its personnel and their operations an effect can be achieved out of all proportion to the numbers and the cost, and far greater than the ability of parties.

For such the prerequisite is the realisation that the gravity and urgency of the struggle makes it tantamount to a war, and that the ubiquity of the menace makes that war a war on all the fronts of life, and thus a total war. Thus, for this spearhead of the struggle politics becomes a whole way of life, not just the fragmentary involvement of the party. One joins the later with a signature and a subscription.

One becomes part of the former by living the cause as a worker and fighter. It follows from this outlook of the vanguard for victory that a high standard of political education, systematic training for present activities, and far-sighted preparation for the future culmination of breakdown, is imperative.

Whereas parties are concerned to talk about the betterment of things after an electoral triumph, the task force is concerned to practice the better life as much as possible now in anticipation of the future formation of government. Hence it is concerned shrewdly to survey and assess the extent to which, even today, the new can be practiced within the frontiers of the old, and thus to that limited but nevertheless substantial extent society can be here and now transformed from within.

This means not only the daily code of living of the isolated individual, but also the coalescence of individuals in residential communities, providing a microcosm of the New Order; or, failing that, business ventures and other functional projects; remembering that, as a side effect, the finest propaganda is provided by an example in practice.

STUDY OF POWER

Such a survey reveals that there is a vast territory of life not subject to either the effective or the attempted control of the enemy. State power is the aim of the party, but beyond that destination lies the introduction of new ways in respect of which coercion has its acute limitations and persuasion its much greater place.

Power is but a means to an end which lies in practice, and practice even now within the state of the enemy is a victorious exercise of power. Within you, given the will and the way as one stepping forth in separation from the masses, lies the potentiality of power in plenty. Power thus needs to be finely analysed as a scientific study, whereby all its various forms and levels become properly distinguished, and open to pursuit, not merely those of local and national government.

Thereby not only the establishment of a special settlement, or the coming together of fellow activists in a density of residential proximity, seen as a sizeable seizure of power, but so too is an act of infiltration by an individual into a position of influence whereby he or she can substantially promote an aspect of our creed detached from an off-putting identification with a total parcel of policy.

An example of a functional project lies in the field of education, where at present in the generality of schooling there is not only an appalling failure to impart the vital knowledge of Race and true history, and to encourage strong and wholesome character with its appreciation of the need for discipline and its sense of service to the folk community; but there is also an intensive corruption by the multi-racialist and Marxist teachers who predominate in the profession today, resulting in a generation alienated from our folk, and in character either soft and spineless or nihilistic and vicious.

Thus, one of the tasks of the task force should be to develop its own schooling and out-of-school training for its children.

All such implantations of the new within the realm of the old order is some contribution to its breakdown, but, beyond this, there are ways galore directly to damage the enemy's apparatus of power, if one makes a study of it. A spanner in the works and sugar in the petrol tank of Democracy goes more to bring about its breakdown than battling for the ballot box.

Another specialty open to an elite are daring and dramatising deeds of propaganda, whereby a well-trained few with a wealth of imagination but little cost can register a strong impact on the masses —whose psyche responds to boldness—useful now in stimulating and focusing discontent, and useful in the future by establishing a: record of leadership in resistance. In this context, when for example one contemplates the hundreds of thousands of man-hours which have gone into distributing party leaflets which nevertheless have reached but a fraction of the population, and doing so commanded but a tiny response, can it be denied that a far smaller and cheaper effort by the right sort of people could have achieved a far greater and more attentive audience through the transmitters of clandestine radio?

For obvious reasons one cannot here go into and must leave to the fertile imagination the wide range of political warfare open essentially to the select few operating on lines comparable to the special units of Otto Skorzeny. This is essentially the domain of the professional soldier of politics with no room for the dilettante or the juvenile desperado. He, and not the party politician or party member will be the one needed and decisive when the breakdown fully arrives, and the naked struggle for state power follows.

Obviously, a task force in all its various divisions is not something for inauguration and recruitment in the same fashion as a party. Instead it calls for private and personal contact whereby there is ample and prior opportunity to size up a person as both thoroughly genuine and really suitable beyond this before any approach is made and any invitation to participate is subsequently extended. A strict separation of the personnel of the overt from those of the underground activities is absolutely essential; and with the latter, furthermore, a separation of its personnel within cells is imperative.

As things are now, our cause is vitiated by the dead-end politics of the party, a proven failure as an instrument of struggle. Let us face up to this, break free from the related fetters of thinking, and forthwith replace it with a task force!

A TRAIN OF THOUGHT

Author's note: This publication is purely fictional. As such it is neither a description of things happening or about to happen, nor an incitement to bring them about.

Peter Bramham, single, 20, insurance clerk, homeward bound for the West Midlands, searched for and found a comparatively vacant portion of the waiting train at Euston Station.

In London for the Saturday to attend his first big meeting of the nationalist organisation he had recently joined, he now settled down to read a copy of the magazine he had bought there. He had barely finished the first article before the only other nearby passenger, a man opposite him partly hidden behind an outstretched copy of the Evening Standard, tossed it on one side, and, in doing so, noticed and fixed his eyes on the cover of Peter's magazine, and then on Peter himself. Perceiving his scrutiny to be observed, an amiable expression spread across his 30-40-year-old face, and he opened conversation with a remark complimentary to the magazine.

Fraternisation proceeded swiftly, and Peter shortly posed the perennial problem of how to make headway more quickly. "Would it be better to try and infiltrate the Conservative Party, already in power, and turn it to our purpose?" he enquired.

The reply he received was that infiltration could only succeed where the field of power was sufficiently open, and not tightly controlled by people keenly on guard against it, and where there was the possibility of a sufficient base of ready sympathy among the rank and file and lower functionaries.

To attempt to change things within the Conservative Party would be a more gigantic, if not impossible task, than to attempt to oust it from power by external means because of the overwhelming presence in it of the precise mentality responsible for Britain's plight, and a leadership representative of this mentality at its very worst, keenly alert to any threat to person and policy from infiltration.

Peter turned to another argument: "Wouldn't it be wiser not to add so greatly to our difficulties by defending Hitler's Germany of 50 years ago, which is irrelevant to Britain today?"

Answered the older man, "The condition of Britain today, causing her condition in the future, is the product of her past, and thus, shaped by her catastrophic conflict with the only force in history which has really challenged the whole process of Aryan decline. There lies the relevance!

"Our indictment of the old parties would be hugely incomplete, if we omitted to show their wrongs of today in the causal context of their wrongs of a half-century ago.

"The subject of that time past cannot be avoided in principle or in practice. To seek refuge in silence is impossible. To deny relevance is unbelievable. To tender some feeble commentary concurring with the lies of the enemy is disgraceful. The only remaining option is to summon up the courage and integrity to tell the truth."

"However hotly that truth is rejected now, it may be remembered to your credit in the future that you told it, but, regardless of present or future acceptance, the telling of it is of crucial importance to you as an expression of your unflinching determination to face up to the rigours of the great struggle confronting you.

"Consideration of the present public reaction to what you say now on this subject is unimportant because of the enemy's present control of public reaction in general which is well-nigh total, ensuring your overall rejection in any case. Such is the efficacy of the enemy's mind-shaping of the masses by the media it monopolizes, that you could distribute leaflets and hold meetings till you died of old age without causing more than some relatively trifling reverberations which the enemy could easily contain.

DISTRESS: THE MAKER OF CHANGE

"Dire discomfort mixed with the prospect of remedial upheaval is the vital chemistry for the crucible of radical change. This alone can provide the means to jolt the masses out of their induced somnambulism. When, and only when this revolutionary situation arrives will the masses become capable of looking freshly and freely on what you say and what they remember you having said. In that time of change denunciation from the old parties will become recommendation in their ears. Till then, even if you echo the enemy's denigration of Adolf Hitler's crusade for racial salvation, you will never compete successfully with the precedence the old parties command in the public mind because of their powers of presentation; and they will still smear you by associating your basic principles with Hitler, so your contortions to avoid this will be a failure"

Peter persisted in probing for an easier way. "Wouldn't it make things easier, if we attempted a Christian approach?"

"Impossible," re-joined his critic. "All the enfeebling arguments and sentiments of today, responsible for all of today's harmful practices, come to us in their ultimate justification and derivation from Judaic Christianity. They constitute, however vaporous and unidentified, the corpus of the Christian tradition of myth and morality permeating the public regardless of whether the people are practicing or even professing Christians.

"Thus, Britain's parlous political and social condition springs from a spiritual disorder caused by an alien implantation. For this sickness of the soul naturally no ordinary political or social remedy can suffice. What is required is no less than the complete eradication of the cause of this disease, and this by Christianity's entire replacement by an Aryan religion resulting from a Weltanschauung encompassing the whole purpose and all the corresponding values of Aryan existence, and thus supplying it with its requisite totality of vision."

Considerably taken aback by this shock to his conventional deferences, Peter paused a while before it occurred to him to ask about the role of the royal family. Thereupon it was put to him that, doing nothing to oppose the racial ruination of Britain, and instead presiding over it with pomp and circumstance, the royal family cannot rightly be regarded as any manifestation of or focal point for surviving national spirit. Instead they have to be seen as the stars of a soap opera of pseudo-patriotism constantly and glutinously projected by the media to distract and lull the masses while the racial ruination decreed by their masters' proceeds. In this role they are themselves major malefactors in a crime of crimes against our race and nation.

"Nevertheless," said Peter, "even if the public is wrong regarding Hitler's Germany, Christianity, and the royal family, surely, we need public support in order to gain power, and therefore need to conform sufficiently to the thoughts and feelings of the public to get that support?"

"My contention," responded his companion, "is that public support is neither sufficiently obtainable now, even as mere passive approval, nor, as positive action, obtainable in decisive magnitude at any time. Public support, therefore, cannot be the key to power for us."

REALITIES OF POWER-SEEKING

"The objective must be clearly discerned and sharply defined as the attainment of power by any means whatsoever; except those that bring about a functional disability respecting our ultimate aims. This means the attainment of power with or without majority approval beforehand. Majority approval cannot be obtained beforehand because of our lack of the power of the media.

Even if it could be obtained beforehand, it would not be decisive because of the unchangeable nature of the masses which causes them to be incapable of sustained political action as distinct from passive approval or disapproval, and thus incapable of providing the motive force for an electoral attainment of power, or its attainment by any other means. Minorities always have decided things and always will decide things in the final analysis. Even the conventional political party, ostensibly an instrument of the masses, always resolves down into a minority as far as deciding and doing is concerned" .

"This does not mean that public approval is always inconsequential. On the contrary, it is indispensable after the attainment of power, although not so beforehand, and this because the attainment of power is not the end, but only the means whereby a change can be brought about not merely in the workings of the system, but in the whole character of society and the way of life, and for which it is necessary to change the people as far as their nature allows, and in order to do this to secure their cooperation through their approval. The attainment of power will alone give us the power of the media whereby to secure this approval.

"Clearly you cannot work towards this ultimate aim of the revolutionary change necessary for Aryan survival, revival, and advancement, by changing yourself to conform to the pattern of thought and behaviour opposed to this which is imposed on the public by the present masters of the media. This would be to cooperate in your own cancellation, and for the sake of the unsuccessful pursuit of the will-o'-the-wisp of unobtainable public support."

The train slowed to a stop in a station, and the milling throng on the platform caused the older man to exclaim "There you have them: the denizens of democracy, content with the illusion fed to them that they decide things, whereas in reality things are decided for them through their conditioning by the media as to what to accept or reject, according to the dictates of the ultimate and permanent rulers in the background.

"Stuffed with all the permissible thoughts conducive to our downfall; drawn in their millions to devotion to the box, the booze, and the ball, and the pursuit of the pecuniary and plastic pleasures of a society conceived as a supermarket; trained to eschew as antiquarian absurdity anything in the way of heroic idealism: can you really expect salvation to come from the thought and action of these programmed helots?"

DEMOCRACY'S DEATH RATTLE

There intruded from further down the carriage snatches of the devilish din described as "rock," delivered by a midget radio clutched affectionately by one of a couple of long-haired louts clad in tatty jeans. "This is what we are up against!" he added: "the bulk of our younger generation clad appropriately in the slovenly uniform of the creed of slovenliness, debauching their minds in an ecstasy of adoration of a chaos of cacophony and the vile creatures of the night purveying it. This represents democracy's maturity, and that maturity is the prelude to communism."

While not disposed to contest the condemnation, Peter nevertheless, felt obliged to suggest that, if we are concerned to destroy the existing order, surely this makes a case for making use of all elements rebellious to it, such as football hooligans, skinheads, and the "rock against communism" groups adopted by some nationalist bodies.

The reply he got was that a careful distinction had to be made and maintained between simply taking advantage of all disruption to the system by whoever and whatever caused, and, on the other hand, actually associating with and thereby endorsing what are really manifestations of democracy in its dance to death.

Such elements are opposed by nature to all discipline and authority. Accordingly, they would be just as rebellious to a new order. The disruption which we ourselves engage in must be specifically, that which is wrought by discipline and authority for the ultimate triumph of the same.

Talk of "rock against communism" is an absurdity, he was told. "Rock" is the reduction of music to a mass of discordant, crudely repetitive and consequently massively ugly noises. That is communism in sound, communism being the reduction of people to the crude equality of a herd of cattle, and as such the culmination of democracy which is avowedly based on evaluation by numbers.

He paused, and then proceeded with his thesis that the ballot box is not the source but the expression of power.

"You cannot convert the masses without control of either the instruments which have corrupted them, or comparable ones, and you can only gain that through a seizure of state power, since you cannot attain state power by any solicitation of votes. The ballot box today is the response-meter of the television box, and whoever controls the latter box controls the former. National elections now, in this age of mass manipulation by television, are not the means to power for the system's outsiders. Instead, they have become in effect merely the closed shop of permitted opinions, left, right, and centre, put to public endorsement by the system's insiders as the trick whereby to excite and display contentment with its enforcement of conformity, and thus to safeguard its continuation.

ELECTIONS: THE CAMOUFLAGE OF POWER

"Democracy's voting game is thus democracy's confidence trick. The real arbiter is, always has been and always will be the possessor of power already, power used to procure votes, not power procured by votes. The present possessors of ultimate power, where distinct from puppet politicians, attained it or did their predecessors or ancestors by seizure, not by ballot, and they can be relied upon to unite, regardless of tolerable factional differences which are always minor relative to their common interest in the system, in using whatever force in their power to prevent any conceivable access to that power through the ballot box by any conceivable party of our beliefs. Therefore, instead of the pointless pursuit of votes, we have to promote disillusionment with the voting game as an essential part of our true task which is a seizure of power from the syndicates of the system."

"But how on earth can this be done?" objected Peter. "If democracy's political mafia has such tremendous power, including the power to hold the public mind in servitude and so virtually rig elections, how can we, a tiny minority of political outcasts, overcome that enemy?"

"The power structure of the enemy, enormous as it is, is yet far from invulnerable," said the other. "The purposes of social and racial transformation pursued by the enemy—with the aim of absolute security of supremacy by way of a mongrelized flock of sheep—present the possibility of acute public discontent which, while not making the masses into regular activists, can yet cause spasmodic public disorder damaging to, the system. We have to encourage all such discontent contributory to its breakdown.

"Secondly, the system is vulnerable throughout to disruptive attacks aimed at powerfully promoting its natural tendency to breakdown which alone is the situation in which an actual seizure of power can take place. We have with ruthless logic to accept that only through a breakdown can there be a breakthrough for us. Accordingly, we have to concentrate on bringing it about in every possible way, consistent with the core of our ideology."

BREAK THROUGH BY BREAKDOWN

"What do you mean by disruptive attacks?" interrupted Peter.

"Just consider," declared the stranger, "all the ramifications and complexities of the administration of the modern state, and imagine how small but highly competent teams could by one form of action or another seriously upset the mechanism! The subject is a huge study in itself, leading to a veritable science of its own. Visualise this disruption going on for a long time with cumulative effect in the dislocation of services and resulting public discontent! Then visualize the progressive breakdown reaching a stage where the television relay stations are put out of action and the screens go blank, depriving the agitated masses of their diversions and indoctrination! You are then looking at the requisite revolutionary situation for a feasible seizure of the key points of state control."

"Is this project purely clandestine?" asked Peter.

"No," came the answer. "There are formations which can by their nature, and should to their convenience remain overt, such as some for research and some for direct propaganda, as well as communities created to put the new order into practice partially and in miniature for experiment and for example as well as the immediate benefit of those concerned. Such overt formations must necessarily have no overt links whatsoever with the clandestine formations, and even among themselves will best be only secretly linked to one another, and as self-contained as possible to avoid or make difficult multiple suppression when the old order becomes that desperate.

The criterion for the task force is thus not its categorical confinement to clandestine activities, but its categorical confinement in all its activities to a true elite because this alone is competent to conduct successfully the precise activities envisaged.

"I have just mentioned direct propaganda to the public. By that I mean both its overt form and also its covert form, which latter embraces both expressions ruled illegal for its content by such as the Public Order legislation, and also expression held illegal because of its means of communication, such as a network of secret local radio transmitters for the devastating interruption of the sound track of television programmes.

"This is a field of activity for which only the select personnel of the task force are suitable, and which in the extent of its audience and the incisiveness of its impact exceeds all the immensity of man hours of leafleting and street-corner haranguing by conventional nationalist parties.

"Such direct propaganda, I must emphasise, is purely for the twin purpose of creating public discontent, and inspiring potential recruits for the task force, not for recruiting the public into some organisation of the masses which is the folly of the conventional political party."

"Some of the task force activities would be treated as illegal by the present authorities, and used as a pretext for banning the whole thing with public approval," objected Peter. "Wouldn't it be better to stay completely legal, thereby putting the enemy in the wrong before the public, if they nevertheless ban it?"

BANNING BY INSTALMENT PLAN

"You have accurately to know your enemy," responded the other. "Within the whole scheme of deception which is democracy, the stratagem of suppression preferred by the enemy is to prohibit by impediment while pretending that freedom prevails. In keeping with this they are already banning law-abiding racial nationalists and National Socialists by bit-by-bit restriction, such the Public Order legislation preventing racial free speech, and imposing other obstacles, and by the wide-ranging denial of facilities without which rights mean nothing.

"This piecemeal suppression they will assuredly proceed with, even until the effect is virtually total—thereby achieving all that an outright and outspoken ban could achieve, without any of conceivable disadvantage of its directness—depending not how law- abiding you are, but precisely how much of a menace you have become. Any absent and needed pretext will be fabricated without hesitation. The brainwashed British public so far remained unmoved by the denial of freedom to you, can be confidently expected to remain so out of either ignorance or apathy. Moral justification enough exists already for resorting to means proclaimed unlawful by those disqualified from judgement by their contravention of the supreme law of racial survival and their denial to you of the freedom to abide by it. What counts accordingly is not your spurious rating by the enemy as "legal" or "illegal," but your actual ability to hit and overthrow those who have made rebellion for the sake of your race and nation not merely your right but your duty, and conformity to their law an offence against nature."
"What sort of persons would be needed for this task force?" Peter asked next.

Back came the reply: "Those and those alone who are wholly devoted to the survival and advancement of the Aryan folk, perceiving this cause in its fullness and serving it in its entirety through a fusion of the qualities of a trinity of worker, warrior, and priest. As a worker I mean someone applying himself or herself methodically and constantly to the study and other preparation necessary for successful action. As a warrior I mean someone responsive to the commanding fact that the significance of life is struggle, and high achievement in life the heroic waging of that struggle. As a priest I mean someone in whom the well-spring of being and thus the source of a conquering superiority in strength is the perception of the cause in spiritual terms as the pursuit in human affairs of order and harmony reflective of the rational purpose of evolutionary progress measured by the ascendancy of the higher over the lower which is definitive of beauty.

In this pursuit is to be seen a gladsome conformity to the workings and thus the interpreted will of the cosmos discerned thus as divinity; this in essence being the essential new Aryan religion.

"Each such person needs to become superbly fit for whatever tasks in view: physically trained in the martial arts for what is a veritable war; mentally trained in all that needs to be known for those tasks, ranging from a complete comprehension of all aspects of the cause in doctrinal depth and historical context to a full knowledge of the targets and techniques of disruption, and the ways of evading detection and capture, or coping with imprisonment if caught. Alongside this, both to encourage the high degree of teamwork essential and to sustain the individual under all stress, an intense comradeship has to be drawn forth from the triple bond of a racial fellowship, ideological unity, and elitist function. Only such a human weapon of excellence can and will succeed."

"How," queried Peter, "could one contact and join this task force?" Back came the answer that entry would necessarily be by invitation only. "What would happen," said the other, "would be that persons such as yourself, in or outside the ordinary organisations, would be watched at length and checked extensively, and, if and when seen to be thoroughly suitable, then and only then personally approached and invited to join."

At this, Peter's companion, rose and departed, seemingly in the direction of the toilet, but he did not return, and Peter saw nothing more of him—that is, until some two years later when Peter was approached and recruited into Britain's liberation movement, which was then inflicting serious damage on the enemy—but that is another story to be told at another time.

APPENDIX: LETTER TO GERALD KAUFMAN, M.P.

(Editor's note: As this book was being produced, the publisher received word from Colin Jordan that his premises in Yorkshire had been raided by the police. Various political literature was seized, including the nearly complete manuscript of the author's upcoming book Merrie England 2000. The raid, which took place on June 4, 1991, was instigated by Gerald Kaufman, Member of Parliament, on the spurious allegation that Colin Jordan had been sending him anti-Semitic "hate mail" The following is a letter subsequently sent to Mr. Kaufman by Mr. Jordan, which we thought would make a fitting conclusion to this volume.)

Gerald Kaufman M.P.
House of Commons
Westminster
London SW1A OAA

Sir,

    I have been informed by Detective Inspector T.W. Storey of the Harrogate Police that you have laid a complaint against me, alleging that I have sent you a label bearing a cartoon depicting "Uncle Sam" exhorting people to fight for Israel in the recent Middle-East War.
    This allegation, as I have informed the Harrogate Police, is an untrue, malicious and mischievous one; and I have accordingly laid a complaint against you on this score.
    I am of course well aware of your devious purpose behind this stratagem of false complaint. You believe that, while lurking cosily in the background, you can by means of your status as an M.P, and by the alien and misbegotten provisions of Part III of the 1986 Public Order Act so long and so feverishly agitated for by your kind, bring about a Soviet-style intrusion into my home, and thereby a search for and seizure of my property out of which you hope that some case may be concocted against me and some sort of punishment inflicted on me. Fearing the truth of what I say, you seek to silence me in this tyrannical fashion.

Masquerading in the garments of "freedom and democracy," you and your kind are in fact entirely averse to facing in open and fair controversy any case against the Jewish community in this country of which you are a prominent member.

Instead, you have for years been conspiring to take away from Englishmen their ancient freedom of expression as far as it concerns the Jews, agitating for first one new law and then another to prohibit and penalize such expression in the pretence that it is "racial hatred."

Even with the repressive provisions of the current Public Order Act, you are still not satisfied, and want more, from which it is perfectly apparent that you will never be content until any and all comment on the Jews which is unfavourable is rendered illegal.

In all these endeavours detrimental to English freedom, you and your kind are in fact the most potent cause of the very "anti- Semitism" which you purport to combat, and of this I firmly accuse you here and now; since by those endeavours you will sooner or later, naturally and assuredly, create bitter resentment among more and more people who otherwise might well remain untouched by literature and speeches from my side.

"Hatred"—hatred against those like myself who dare to continue to criticise and condemn you and your kind—is an emotion you and your kind must be well acquainted with through your own plentiful manifestation of it in your campaign for suppression.

You yourself will perhaps be best qualified to discern how far this emanates from the teachings of your Talmud, and how far the current and continuing distribution of this piece of literature with its many and varied vicious references to Gentiles can well be said to contravene Part III of the Public Order Act 1986; although of course, you will have no fear of any enforcement of that Part of that Act against your community by authorities so subservient to your community.

Conceivably through the elaborate espionage apparatus of your community you have already come to know that I have reached a draft stage with a book entitled Merrie England 2000, outlining the hideous shape of things to come in this country, given the ascendancy of such as you; and that therefore this is why this manuscript was with special seal removed by the Police for your protection and comfort.

Be certain, however, that it will be re-drafted if necessary, even if it be ultimately honoured by being scheduled as one of the banned books of Britain!

That, as pretext, you should have complained about the precise item of literature you have done is revealing regarding the arrogant pretensions of you and your kind. The cartoon on it cites two foreign countries, one of them Israel, and in no way refers to the Jews in Britain in any derogatory manner. Unless it is that you identify yourself with one of those foreign countries, Israel, you cannot claim to be involved.

As far as my knowledge goes you have been careful so far not so to identify yourself, but, if you do now come out in the open and so identify, I wish you good speed in implementing that identification by your permanent departure for Israel!

Failing that, you might remember that the Expulsion of the Jews by our good King Edward the First to the universal joy of the nation in 1290 has never yet been formally revoked, and your presence in our land, let alone our Parliament, may therefore be deemed illicit.

As one whose ancestors were tilling the soil of Yorkshire centuries before your most immediate ones came here from the ghettoes of the east—your people taking advantage of ours to aspire to ascendancy over us, and now to censor and silence us—conclude by informing you in relation to your efforts to make patriotism a crime and to incriminate me that by far the greatest criminals in this land today, and indeed the very greatest in our history, are those who have been responsible for allowing and encouraging the coloured invasion of our country, and the forced integration of our people, and responsible for allowing and promoting Jewish ascendancy in it over our affairs.

If you are one such accomplice in this giant crime of betrayal of the British folk, then you are most certainly one of those arch- criminals I have in mind.

Yours sincerely,
Colin Jordan

National Socialism: Vanguard of the Future

BIOGRAPHICAL NOTE

Born 1923. Education leading to the study of history at Cambridge University, 1946-49, there graduating with an Honours Degree. Subsequently a representative for the north of Scotland for a major firm, and then a teacher until banned from teaching because of out-of-school activities. Active in a succession of political organisations between 1946 and 1962, in which latter year founded and led the National Socialist Movement. Imprisoned in 1962 for organising an elite formation in that Movement and for a *"Hitler Was Right!"* speech in London's Trafalgar Square. Again, imprisoned in 1967 for literature on the issues of Jews and Coloured immigration. Headed the British Movement, which replaced the N.S.M. in 1968, till withdrawal from it in 1975 because of personal commitments. Since then he has confined himself to writing and to literature sales.

POSTSCRIPT TO THE 2011 EDITION

After a lifetime of service to his race, John Colin Campbell Jordan passed away on 9 April 2009 at his home north of Harrogate, Yorkshire, aged 86 years.

POSTSCRIPT TO THE 2021 EDITION

12 years on from his death the writings of Colin Jordan continue to inspire a new generation tired of the old establishment systems in their countries. The Covid pandemic has caused many people world-wide to search out a better way for the future and National Socialism offers them that opportunity. Perhaps frightened by this increasing interest in Colin Jordan and his political philosophy the BBC have in 2021 released a 4 part "docu-drama" called "Ridley Road" which deals with Colin Jordan and his National Socialist Movement. Needless to say this "docu-drama" is full of propaganda, half truths, and vile lies. To produce a 4 hour long television programme with the principle aim of attacking the man and his beliefs shows that the establishment is afraid of the growing influence in the writings, of Colin Jordan. This, the largest print run yet, of his works shows that National Socialism is winning the argument and his belief that *"together we can turn the defeat of 1945 into but a lost battle in a continuing war from which we shall emerge victorious"*

National Socialism: Vanguard of the Future

'Twaz a Good Fight! written by Stephen Frost. 336 pages ISBN:9781899765140

In addition to interviewing Jordan on numerous occasions, Frost was given free access to Jordan's voluminous personal archives. He further incorporates into his text fragments from Jordan's unfinished autobiography, *"Before the Sun Goes Down"*. The result is a detailed and sympathetic account of the life of this extraordinary personality.

This and other works are available directly from NS Press (UK) and other booksellers.

Colin Jordan Commemorative Die Struck coin. Available from NS Press (UK)

www.ingramcontent.com/pod-product-compliance
Lightning Source LLC
Chambersburg PA
CBHW071531080526
44588CB00011B/1636